Major Arcana Cards from The Llewellyn Tarot
by Anna-Marie Ferguson

0 The Fool

1 The Magician

2 The Priestess

3 The Empress

4 The Emperor

5 The Hierophant

6 The Lovers

7 The Chariot

8 Strength

9 The Hermit

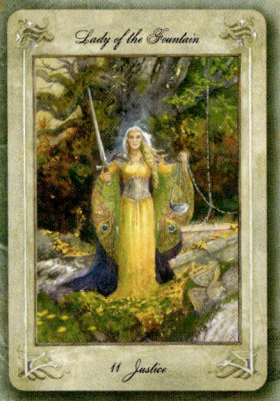

About the Author

Ly de Angeles is a tarot consultant with a local, national, and international clientele. She has taught tarot and similar subjects for many years. Her reputation for uncanny and startling accuracy has spread by word of mouth rather than advertising. She is high priestess of the coven of Wildwood Gate, whose members are spread around the world, and she has been involved in the occult arts and sciences since being introduced to them when she was a young girl. She lives in Australia. Her other books published by Llewellyn include *Witchcraft: Theory and Practice*, *When I See the Wild God*, and novels *The Quickening* and *The Shining Isle*.

To Write to the Author

If you wish to contact the author or would like more information about this book, please write to the author in care of Llewellyn Worldwide and we will forward your request. Both the author and publisher appreciate hearing from you and learning of your enjoyment of this book and how it has helped you. Llewellyn Worldwide cannot guarantee that every letter written to the author can be answered, but all will be forwarded. Please write to:

Ly de Angeles
℅ Llewellyn Worldwide
2143 Wooddale Drive, Dept. 978-0-7387-1138-6
Woodbury, Minnesota 55125-2989, U.S.A.
Please enclose a self-addressed stamped envelope for reply,
or $1.00 to cover costs. If outside U.S.A., enclose
international postal reply coupon.

Many of Llewellyn's authors have websites with additional information and resources. For more information, please visit our website at http://www.llewellyn.com

TAROT
THEORY & PRACTICE

A Revolutionary Approach to How the Tarot Works

Ly de Angeles

Llewellyn Publications
Woodbury, Minnesota

Tarot Theory & Practice: A Revolutionary Approach to How the Tarot Works © 2007 by Ly de Angeles. All rights reserved. No part of this book may be used or reproduced in any manner whatsoever, including Internet usage, without written permission from Llewellyn Publications except in the case of brief quotations embodied in critical articles and reviews.

First Edition
First Printing, 2007

Cover Texture © Brand X, Card image is from the Llewellyn Tarot. Artist: Anna Marie Ferguson
Cover design by Gavin Dayton Duffy
Editing by Connie Hill
Interior card images from the Llewellyn Tarot. Artist: Anna Marie Ferguson
Interior illustrations provided by the author and redrawn by the Llewellyn Art Department, except on page 31, *Infinity's Web* by Bernard Casimir used with permission.

Llewellyn is a registered trademark of Llewellyn Worldwide, Ltd.

Library of Congress Cataloging-in-Publication Data

De Angeles, Ly, 1951–
  Tarot theory and practice : a revolutionary approach to how the tarot works / Ly de Angeles. -- 1st ed.
      p. cm.
  Includes bibliographical references and index.
  ISBN 978-0-7387-1138-6 (alk. paper)
  1. Tarot. I. Title.
  BF1879.T2D364   2007
  133.3'2424—dc22
                                                                                            2007026249

Llewellyn Worldwide does not participate in, endorse, or have any authority or responsibility concerning private business transactions between our authors and the public.
  All mail addressed to the author is forwarded but the publisher cannot, unless specifically instructed by the author, give out an address or phone number.
  Any Internet references contained in this work are current at publication time, but the publisher cannot guarantee that a specific location will continue to be maintained. Please refer to the publisher's website for links to authors' websites and other sources.

Llewellyn Publications
A Division of Llewellyn Worldwide, Ltd.
2143 Woodale Drive, Dept. 978-0-7387-1138-6
Woodbury, Minnesota 55125-2989, U.S.A.
www.llewellyn.com

Printed in the United States of America

Other Books by This Author

FROM LLEWELLYN PUBLICATIONS
Witchcraft: Theory and Practice
When I See the Wild God
The Quickening
The Shining Isle

FROM WILDWOODGATE
The Feast of Flesh and Spirit
Genesis: Legend of Future Past

FROM UNITY/PRISM, UK
The Way of the Goddess
The Way of Merlyn

Tarot

Ominous...
This built-up haze of rage upon a people!
Weave softly through it . . .
They do not know I taste them when they're lying;
On the surface they pretend, inside they're dying
And all the while they say how hard they're trying
But trying doesn't work—to live you do it!

They fear me for I tell them what they're hiding
Deep beneath the well-kept faces of the young;
I tell them every buried song unsung;
Every sight and every slander of the tongue;
Of the hell into which, slowly, they are sliding.

I am Tarot; revolution . . .
I'm the Raven that sits, and whispers, on your shoulder;
I can name the savage beast that lurks behind you;
I'm the mirror of the Thing you hope won't find you
And you fear me, for I cannot but remind you
That you're older now . . . and will get so much older.

She comes to see herself in my reflection
In the hope that I will tell her nothing's wrong;
That behind the weak betrayal she is strong;
That she can change the places where she can't belong . . .
That she can handle life without love's lost affection.

How I want to set them free;
See them treat life tenderly;
Have them know that they are me!

Malevolent . . .
The stealing hand of "How do I survive?"
That chokes him like the grief of Lilith's daughter;
That takes his breath away and makes him fear;
"Is there anybody," begs he softly, "who can hear?
Someone who won't make me 'goat-to-slaughter'?
Because I'm drowning but I cannot see the water."

I beg them "Dance;"
I cry "Alive!"
I scream out "Live it more,
don't merely just survive!
You have the Name of it within—
to waste life *is* the only sin . . .
to taste the holy bloody feast of life's creation
is your first and last—and *only*—obligation."

I am the song of you that calls you to awaken;
the archer and the bow, not just the arrow.
She speaks for me, but I am *you*, forsaken;
I *am* you, always was, down to the marrow—
the deep and ancient future,
        I am Tarot.

Contents

Introduction . . . xiii
The Twelve-Unit Syllabus in Brief . . . xv

Part One—The Theory of Everything

Unit One: Time and Multiple Reality . . . 3
Theory: The First Barrier—De-conditioning the Common Paradigm . . . 3
Practice: A Simple Visualization . . . 7
Theory: Tarot and the Theory of the Big Bang . . . 8
Practice: Y-node Theory . . . 9
The Chicken or the Egg—Collapsing the Wave . . . 11
Light and Thought . . . 11
Raziel . . . 16

Unit Two: What Tarot Is and What It Isn't . . . 21
Minimalist History . . . 21
Practice: The Personal Energetic Field and Body Language . . . 22

Unit Three: Who Defines 'Reality'? . . . 25
Theory: Shadow Reality/Multiple Reality and Alternative Lives . . . 25
Multiple Lives: Ourselves in the Future, Our Connection with Many Gods—
Close Encounters of the Second Kind . . . 26
To Die, or Not to Die, That Is the Question . . . 27
Shadow Reality . . . 34
Free Will and Fate . . . 36
The Random Factor . . . 38

Part Two—Tarot, the Living Tradition

Unit Four: Communication and Perception . . . 41
Practice: Communication vs. Babble . . . 41
Practice: Learning Objectivity—What Do You Really See? . . . 42

Unit Five: From Evolution to Current World Events . . . 45
Theory: The Tree of Life . . . 45
Back to the Future (The Theory of Evolution) . . . 47
Microcosmically . . . 47
Macrocosmically . . . 49
Practice: The Making of a Template and First Use of Major Arcana . . . 59

Unit Six: The Infinite and the Individual . . . 63
Theory: From No-thing to Something—The Individual and the Tree of Life . . . 63
The Individual . . . 64
Practice: Using the Template and All Cards to Decode Individual and Public Events . . . 70

Unit Seven: The Soul's Journey . . . 71
Theory: The Major Arcana and the Cycles of the Personal Tree of Life . . . 71
Practice: Where Am I Now? . . . 86

Unit Eight: The 78 Cards and Their Meanings . . . 89
Theory: The Major Arcana—Meanings . . . 89
The Minor Arcana—Meanings . . . 112
Time Sequences—Represented by the Pages . . . 168

Part Three—Practicing Your Craft

Unit Nine: The First Nine Months . . . 171
Preparation . . . 171
Practice Aloud . . . 172
The Opening Ritual and the 3-Card Read . . . 172
Needing Willing Allies . . . 173

Unit Ten: Tarot Spreads . . . 175
Section 1: Theory . . . 175
Spread 1—The Celtic Cross (Present, Future, Past) . . . 176
Spread 2—General Events . . . 179
Spread 3—Other People and Specific Events ("Every 7th Card" Spread 1) . . . 180
Spread 4—Tree of Life . . . 181

Spread 5—Warning . . . 184
Spread 6—Anything Else . . . 184
Spread 7—Destiny . . . 185
Spread 8—Question . . . 185
Section 2: Two Examples of Full Consultations . . . 186
Example 1: Consultation for 'Jane Smith'—The Queen of Wands . . . 189
Example 2: Consultation for 'John Brown'—the King of Wands (Media) . . . 207

Part Four—The Future

Unit Eleven: Understanding the Way . . . *225*

Theory: Tarot Itself as Teacher—Personal Detachment . . . 225
Divining for Yourself or Those Close to You . . . 232
The Fear Factor: Telling Bad News . . . 232
The Spoken Word: The Literal Truth . . . 235
The Plateau . . . 237
Myth and Legend: The Morality of Tarot . . . 237

Unit Twelve: Going Professional . . . *239*

Walking the Walk . . . 239
Transference . . . 242
The Code of Silence and Selective Memory . . . 243
First Do No Harm . . . 244
Client Contact and the Consultation . . . 245
Self-Protection and Psychic Clag . . . 247
The "He/She's My Best Friend" Syndrome and Personal Privacy . . . 248
"Should's": You Won't See What Is Not Realized . . . 249
Safety and Responsibility: Some Dos and Don'ts . . . 250

Wrapping Things Up . . . *253*
Appendix: Meanings with Other Cards . . . *257*
Annotated Bibliography . . . *287*
Recommended Reading and Internet References . . . *291*

Introduction

I have been interpreting Tarot for thirty years and teaching it for twenty.

Realizing that there are a plethora of books available on the subject has meant that I have neglected giving you my own teaching technique, not wanting to add simply one more stick onto the pile.

But it's time. This is the book I have always said I would/could never write. I learned these techniques, initially, through an oral tradition and over the years that is also how I have taught it, and I have needed to become sufficiently competent as a writer to attempt this!

I teach what are called *Walking the Web—Tarot Collectives* on average every six months, with never more than ten students in each class, who train intensively for eight hours a day, one day a week for ten weeks, always with copious homework. While many have gone on to become competent readers, there are also many who decided it was too big a risk to their personal lives and were simply pleased to have acquired the metaphysical knowledge and understanding.

Some of you will become accomplished in this art, but many of you will not, as not everyone *can* become a Tarot reader. That's okay, because it's better to learn as much as you can, do the training and experiment, but also to be comfortable with yourself if it doesn't end up being your thing.

When Tarot becomes aware of you and you change in accordance with *its* nature (and never the other way around) you *become* Tarot. This process begins with the realization that nothing is separate—that everything is a unique expression of the Whole that is life, the universe, and everything—is the ultimate, ultimate liberation!

Part One will focus primarily on breaking down traditional understandings of such things as time, matter, and energy, how prophecy works, the laws of cause and effect, and certain imperative understandings such as language and literality; the implications of divination to the practitioner and the public; responsibility, and objectivity. There are a few exercises in this section.

Part Two discusses the Tree of Life and *its* relationship to life—both macrocosmically and microcosmically—and, as the glyph of this system is used as the central theme of a client consultation, this deeper knowledge is integral.

You will then progress to the relationship between the Tree of Life, Astrology, and Tarot until we arrive at the information on the Major Arcana and the Soul's Journey. From there you will gain a definitive understanding of all the cards, and the keywords necessary for interpretation.

Part Three is your practice workshop and *Part Four* is a guide to going professional.

I have broken the work down into units so that you can take your time studying. There are twelve altogether. You can progress as slowly or as quickly as you choose, but these twelve units represent a symbolic twelve-month training process.

It is advisable to purchase your pack of Tarot cards before you begin the program as you will be using the deck throughout our time together. We won't be using the cards initially, but it is good to familiarize yourself with the images and find the box or make the bag that you will keep them in to keep them away from others' hands (most necessary).

Working as a Group

It will be of enormous benefit to do the following series of workshops with an interested friend, or friends, as working in a group can trigger plenty of healthy debate, opinion, and clarity. It will aid you in backing up each other's objectivity and assist all concerned to remember the rather large quantity of information. It will also serve later, when practicing the spreads, to have a ready group willing to experiment with each other before going out into the wider community.

If I find myself talking to you as though you are a group, please bear with me (and hopefully that's exactly what you will have set up).

The Twelve-Unit Syllabus in Brief

Part One—The Theory of Everything
Unit One: Time and Multiple Reality
We live in conscious ignorance of our immortality.

- *The First Barrier—De-conditioning the Common Paradigm*—breaks down conditioned considerations of time; covers different calendars, discusses biological time, psychological time, physical time, and opens up concepts of infinite time, eradicating consensual limitations.

- *A Simple Visualization*—allows you to consider two things at the same time.

- *Tarot and the Theory of the Big Bang*—is a generalized understanding of this theory discussing the possibility of how information is imparted from the client to the reader through the medium of the cards.

- *Y-Node Theory*—is a written exercise in understanding the infinite.

- *The Chicken or the Egg: Collapsing the Wave*—asks the question "What if the events predicted through the Tarot would never have occurred if they had not been predicted?" which leads us to the next point.

- *Light and Thought*—is a discussion on what thought is, how it can cause things to manifest, and how Tarot's predictions work by way of this understanding. This section also gives some of the many reasons why clients will seek you out and the processes involved.

Unit Two: What Tarot Is and What It Isn't
What Tarot isn't, is just a pack of 78 cards.

- *Minimalist History*—discusses the difference between cards and Tarot.

- *The Personal Energetic Field and Body Language*—is a series of experimentations through both observation and interaction with others.

Unit Three: Who Defines 'Reality'?
Were events predicted by Tarot already in existence somewhere?

- *Shadow Reality/Multiple Reality and Alternative Lives*—asks you questions in relation to how prediction works.

- *Multiple Lives: Ourselves in the Future, Our Connection with Many Gods*—Close Encounters of the Second Kind—discusses how entities, gods, and other unseen presences make contact and guide us through life.

- *To Die, or Not to Die, that Is the Question*—considers what death isn't and introduces the Tree of Life in an initial understanding of continuum, parallel lives, and the presence of the dead at a consultation.

- *Shadow Reality*—discusses how we can live more lives than one in the same incarnation and also looks at the "What is my purpose in life?" question.

- *Free Will and Fate*—looks deeply into whether there is choice in anything.

- *The Random Factor*—mentions the Fool Card and how information is hidden from both the reader and the client.

Part Two—Tarot, the Living Tradition
Unit Four: Communication and Perception
The more you take note of this inner Voice the more it will communicate.

- *Communication vs. Babble*—is an experiment in listening (internally and externally) and setting up situations to test your findings.

- *Learning Objectivity: What Do You Really See?*—is an exercise in peripheral observation.

Unit Five: From Evolution to Current World Events

With all magical training it is important to initially learn as much as one can.

- *The Tree of Life*—begins the understanding of a vast system of knowledge on continuum and the model of the stylized glyph of the Tree is given an organic understanding relevant to the preceding units and describes the continuing prediction of the future of the earth (as we know it) using this model.

- *Back to the Future (The Theory of Evolution)*—is the glyph of the Tree of Life and its implications.

- *Microcosmically*—discusses the Tree of Life in relation to an individual organism.

- *Macrocosmically*—theorizes evolution by way of the template.

- *The Making of a Template and First Use of Major Arcana*—gets you drawing the model for yourself, including all relevant associations, and using the Major Arcana for the first time.

Unit Six: The Infinite and the Individual

It is as much your personal family tree as it is the movement of global cultures.

- *From No-thing to Something: The Tree of Life as an Individual*—first asks you to consider the given concepts in an endless fashion rather than a stylized model, then goes on to give the relationship between the Tree of Life and three aspects of the individual: body, soul, and spirit.

- *The Individual.*

- *The Template and All Cards to Decode both Individual and Public Events*—uses the entire pack of cards here in the Tree of Life layout: ". . . when you have laid them out you will not know exactly *who* the sequence represents! They can be telling you information about anyone from your best friend to the president of a country . . . even the fate of a country itself."

Unit Seven: The Soul's Journey

. . . individual, family, or nation through . . . seemingly treacherous times.

- *The Major Arcana and the Cycles of the Personal Tree of Life*—utilizes the Major Arcana in a given format to allow you to see the unfolding pattern of a life cycle; a natural progression that can often be confusing if not understood. It is a guide to understanding the alchemy of personal transformation.

- *Where Am I Now?*—implements all the cards in the pattern described in the previous section to gauge your current cycle. Examples are given to aid in the interpretation.

Unit Eight: The 78 Cards and Their Meanings
. . . don't be so rigid as to insist interpretations have only these meanings.

- *The Major Arcana: Meanings*—covers many meanings of these cards depending on context.
- *The Minor Arcana: Meanings*—covers many meanings of these cards depending on context.
- *Time Sequences*—shows how Tarot can supply exact timing of events.

Part Three—Practicing Your Craft
Unit Nine: The First Nine Months
. . . lubed your psyche and consciousness like oil on a rusty hinge.

- *Preparation*—talks about acquiring your pack and other materials and setting up your personal work space, and it includes the following:
- *Practice Aloud*—where you establish your verbal interaction with Tarot.
- *The Opening Ritual and the 3-Card Read*—where you learn to open the pack for a reading and begin a journal based on a daily interpretation of three cards only.
- *Needing Willing Allies*—begins your reading for others and asking their assistance in your training.

Unit Ten: Tarot Spreads—Application of Spreads in a Real-life Scenario
You will need to watch carefully how the deck is cut.

Section 1: Theory
I am using eight spreads for each consultation. This is excessive for a beginner, but I prefer to give you as much information as possible for you to adapt for yourselves as you progress.

The spreads used in a consultation are:

- *The Celtic Cross.*
- *General Events.*
- *Other People and Specific Events.*
- *The Tree of Life.*

- *The Warning*—same layout as Other People and Specific Events.
- *Anything Else*—the same layout as the Celtic Cross.
- *Destiny (Tree of Life: Ruach)*—Major Arcana Only.
- *Question*—same layout as the Celtic Cross. When you get around to interpreting this spread (you may allow more than one question to your clients) I have given as much advice on the quirkiness of the process as possible without supplying an example spread.

Section 2: Two Examples of Full Consultations

These include two consecutive consultation examples utilizing all eight spreads, with both brief example interpretations and in-depth breakdowns of card clusters. Each is based solely on one client at a time to allow you to see the continuum as the consultations progress.

- *Example 1: Consultation for "Jane Smith"*—The Queen of Wands.
- *Example 2: Consultation for "John Brown"*—King of Wands (Media).

Part Four—The Future
Unit Eleven: Understanding the Way
There is no Tarot without Magic.

- *Tarot Itself as Teacher—Personal Detachment*—discusses the changing nature of time and how impossible, for example, it would have been a hundred years ago to predict such things as nuclear proliferation or nano-technology and the need to be alert to what Tarot will expose over time. There are examples and case histories to aid in this understanding.
- *Divining for Yourself or Those Close to You*—explains the difficulty in reading for those with whom you are well-acquainted.
- *The Fear Factor: Telling Bad News*—discusses how predicting an event can heal because of the nature of destiny (includes case histories).
- *The Spoken Word: The Literal Truth*—explains how the actual words you are guided to use during a session are explicit in the outcome of events (includes case histories).
- *The Plateau*—explains this uncomfortable but inevitable time in your training and career.

- *Myth and Legend: The Morality of Tarot*—discusses the truth of the fact that Tarot does not view the world or events by way of any consensual morality based on either religion or state.

Unit Twelve: Going Professional
"You had best develop a thick skin . . ."

- *Walking the Walk*—guides you through the preferences and pitfalls of going professional, including how to set up a space in which to work under adverse conditions.

- *Transference*—is a personal opinion on how information is transmitted from the client to the reader and how your own experience (both physical and emotional) of the reading will reflect future events.

- *The Code of Silence and Selective Memory*—discusses the ethics of forgetting clients' information.

- *First Do No Harm*—suggests ways of communicating that ensures the client's well-being despite the information.

- *Client Contact and the Consultation*—talks about what you can expect to experience from the moment of contact with the prospective client to the conclusion.

- *Self-Protection and Psychic Clag*—things you will need to do to prevent being overwhelmed or becoming ill from your work (includes case history).

- *The "He/She's My Best Friend" Syndrome and Personal Privacy*—talks about what to do if people cross your personal-privacy line.

- *"Should's": You Won't See What Is Not Realized*—many people will seek for you to make their decisions for you and what you do about this; your necessary boundaries.

- *Safety and Responsibility: Some Dos and Don'ts*—discusses reputation, reiterates a few earlier comments and cautions you on certain situations that could actually be dangerous.

Appendix: Meanings with Other Cards—is where you can study a multitude of card clusters.

Part One
The Theory of Everything

UNIT ONE

Time and Multiple Reality

Theory: The First Barrier—De-conditioning the Common Paradigm

The most beautiful thing we can experience is the mysterious. It is the sower of all true art and all science. He to whom this emotion is a stranger, who can no longer pause to wonder and stand rapt in awe, is as good as dead: his eyes are closed.

—Albert Einstein[1]

Because of Einstein's theories, we often call time the fourth dimension. Special relativity shows that time behaves surprisingly like the three spatial dimensions and that length contracts as speed increases, time expands as speed decreases.

Scientists have been graphing time, as if it were a length, for hundreds of years, but time never *behaves* exactly like a spatial dimension. We seemingly cannot go backward in time, just as we seemingly cannot go forward, but is this necessarily true?

---

1 Source—http://www.spaceandmotion.com/Albert-Einstein-Quotes.htm

The thing I understand about how people think of time is that it's a tool of measurement—from one event or thing to the next and the periods between. It's a tool for keeping appointments, for remembering how old we are, for . . . for just plain remembering.

How, then, did it end up looking like a line? Is it a line? Does our language imprint on our understanding of time?

Examples

Bastille Day, 14 July every year, celebrates the French Revolution.

The Great Pyramid of Cheops was probably built between 2589–2566 BCE.

What do we see?

In both of the above examples we are given dates or years, either historically accurate but misleading in their entirety (as in the first example) or considered relative to a conjectured event—the invention of the Church of Rome as being the beginning of our current era (the second example).

Today is Monday 3 October, 2005. Isn't it? It is on the Gregorian calendar!

- According to the Mayan calendar today is Long count = 12.19.12.12.4; tzolkin = 7 Kan; haab = 2 Yax.
- On the Islamic calendar it's 29 Sha'ban 1426.
- The Hebrew calendar informs us that today is 29 Elul 5765.
- On the old Julian calendar, today is only 20 September 2005.
- The Persian calendar tells us today is 11 Mehr 1384.
- According to the Chinese calendar, our 3 October 2005 is actually Cycle 78, year 22 (Yi-You), month 9 (Bing-Xu), day 1 (Geng-Shen).
- On the Coptic calendar, today is 23 Tut 1722 .
- The Ethiopic system informs us that today is 23 Maskaram 1998.

Added to the above, what I can glean from other sources is that there are at least three ways that the age of the universe can be estimated:

- The age of the chemical elements.
- The age of the oldest star clusters.
- The age of the oldest white dwarf stars.

The age of the chemical elements can be estimated using radioactive decay to determine how old a given mixture of atoms is. The most definite ages that can be determined this way are ages since the solidification of rock samples. When a rock solidifies, the chemical elements often get separated into different crystalline grains in the rock, and when applying this method of measurement to rocks on the surface of the Earth, the oldest rocks are about 3.8 billion years old.

There are many examples of how humans gauge time but (a) are we correct? and (b) what are we trying to prove?

Professor Bradley Dowden (California State University, Sacramento), in his extensive article on time[2], says

> The concept of linear time first appeared in the writings of the Hebrews and the Zoroastrian Iranians. The Roman writer Seneca also advocated linear time. Plato and most other Greeks and Romans believed time to be motion and believed cosmic motion was cyclical, but this wasn't envisioned as requiring any detailed endless repetition such as the multiple rebirths of Socrates. However, the Pythagoreans and some Stoic philosophers did adopt this drastic position.

Time is also, in a more localized way, understood as:

- Biological time
- Psychological time
- Physical time

Biological time

While also being subjective, biological time is our perceived view of the lifespan of living organisms. A seed is planted and it germinates, grows leaves, bears fruit, fulfills its allotted purpose, and eventually begins the process of decay. The same process applies to every organism—to all appearances, they seem to die.

Psychological time

The concept is highly subjective. If you are bored with your job, yet you must remain at your desk doing meaningless and repetitive tasks with no sense of challenge or intellectual/emotional stimulation, the clock on the wall can become like an enemy, constantly

---

2 Source—http://www.utm.edu/research/iep/t/time.htm#H1

informing you of your situation. Should you sleep in and be racing to catch a bus, time will, again, be your enemy—racing unnaturally to trap you into the consequences of being late.

Psychological time affects us as we age. How often have you heard the expression "This year has just gone by so fast!" comparing it to past years that, as memory serves, were slower and less demanding.

Physical time

Physical time is based on time-pieces, calendars, measurements from one event to the next, the ages, and historical records.

This gives me the distinct sensation that the calculation of time as we know it is the product of human invention; it is the product of a culture-biased humanity.

Most so-called primitive people utilize calendars based on both solar and lunar seasonal cycles and, as such, relate to time in what I consider a more natural fashion. Crops grow and are harvested, the best seed is replanted in the season known for generations to be most propitious, people and animals live and die, and none of this is considered either disturbing or unnatural.

The introduction of linear time into consciousness seems to be ultimately and irrevocably bound up with the ideology of a beginning, a middle, and an end. This is disturbing. Why? Because the consciousness of a finite reality implies obliteration, and obliteration is impossible.

The truth is that nothing ever goes away. It merely changes. At a quantum level all matter is energy expressing itself in an apparently stable state that is, beneath appearances, utterly unstable. Should, as we are told, our sun become a nova (or supernova, as has been suggested), exploding our little corner of space into a zillion trillion particles of cosmic dust . . . well? It's still there. We're still there. It can't be otherwise! If we take simply the understanding of biological death into consideration, then everything and everyone that has ever died is still here—as the earth upon which we walk, as the air we breath and the water we drink, as the food we eat.

How could it be otherwise?

With this understanding, the idea of an afterlife is not taken into consideration in this book, mainly because there is no such thing—life is life and there is nothing that is *not* life. That doesn't in any way rule out concepts of alternate realities or Otherworlds—it most certainly does not—because many people, including me, have experienced such. It simply rules out endings.

While reading Tarot I have had encounters with so-called dead people that do not consider themselves so. The information that they have passed on to the client is always valid (I will site examples later) and what has become obvious to me through interaction with these people is that none of them are dead! Only the observer considers them so. Only the person who thinks of their loved one as dead considers them so.

It is imperative that the student of Tarot enter into the contemplation, and subsequent consciousness-altering understanding, of what time could be, might be, is, and is not, before boxing terminology such as "past," "present," and "future" into an ideology of differences because our responsibility—as interpreters—is to maintain a mind wide open to the ramifications of prophecy.

Practice: A Simple Visualization

The following visualization will assist you to understand where all this is leading:

Find a quiet, peaceful place and sit comfortably, concentrating on breathing into your diaphragm until your breath becomes naturally shallow and calm.

In your mind's eye see a pool of still water and visualize dropping a pebble into the centre of the surface.

Two things:

a. Understand, during the visualization, that the pool is bottomless, and
b. Observe the concentric ripples that expand outward from the centre where they stop at a finite shore.

This is the visualization I use to understand time. The pebble dropping endlessly through the water is as much the reality as the finite surface expression of any event.

So it seems to me regarding *every* observable event. Although they seem to have their place in past, present, or future, there is another aspect to the story—their place in forever.

This leads me to discuss one theory of how prophecy, relative to Tarot, actually works (I can only site my own experience here to avoid conjecture regarding how others say it works), and this can be considered from within the framework of yet another theory called Arrow of Time[3].

---

3 For easy reference: http://www.utm.edu/research/iep/t/time.htm#ARROW

Theory: Tarot and the Theory of the Big Bang

If we take the theory of the big bang, or the moment of the speculated creation of the universe, into account . . . we were there.

Nothing comes from nothing, so of course I do consider that the conceptual big bang could simply have been another universe passing through an infinitely small orifice, or sound generating a material expression, or the superposition of two mutually opposing waves somewhere beyond the known universe, or an exploding/imploding singularity. On the other hand, it could have easily occurred because some young god wanted to experiment, in some far-flung corner of his mother's laboratory, with a project that may or may not have been dangerous.

We were still there; otherwise we would not be here now. Inherent in the DNA of every living thing is the existing memory of all that has preceded its current host (self). The iron in our hemoglobin is still the original iron, the hydrogen molecules within our body's water are still the same hydrogen as is every other element and compound that makes us *us*. The knowledge has been passed to us from our biological parents, to them from theirs, and so on all the way along the Arrow of Time, even before we were, theoretically, amoeba in a soup of one-celled creatures floating in the viscous seas of Infant Earth with no discernible differences to blowflies or elephants.

This theory of the origins of Earth introduces us to our mothers and our fathers and our DNA remembers them (re-member: to re-embody that which has come before).

We are so conditioned to think that our lives began with our births and will end with our deaths (no matter the belief, or lack of it, in an afterlife) that we do life an abysmal injustice. We live in conscious ignorance of our immortality.

So the theory is that when an individual shuffles the cards that represent Tarot, they actually unconsciously sort them into effective order—an impossibility to do consciously—that something other than randomness is most definitely involved (occasionally random elements can enter into a reading, but there are reasons for that which I will cover later in *Shadow Reality—the Random Factor and Alternative Lives*). This supposed shuffle is akin to an accomplished pianist playing Rachmaninoff's Piano Concerto No. 2 in C Minor—he or she certainly does not have to think about what each individual finger is doing or about which note goes where. After much practice the performance is effortless—compartmentalizing each of the components would make it impossible to play.

Every individual has had at least since the big bang to practice.

Practice: Y-Node Theory

To gain an understanding of not only how time *doesn't* go in a straight line but how we could understandably get caught up in the concept of it doing so, you will require a rather large piece of graph paper, a pencil, and, most likely, an eraser.

It should begin as something like the illustration below (figure 1).
Where it ends should surprise you . . .

Each pair of branches that extend away from you extends deeper into time (the past?) and represents a pair of your ancestors. I haven't yet discovered how to make a 3D image of this, but I get the exquisite feeling that it would create an ever-expanding spiral, somewhat like the appearance of a double-helix!

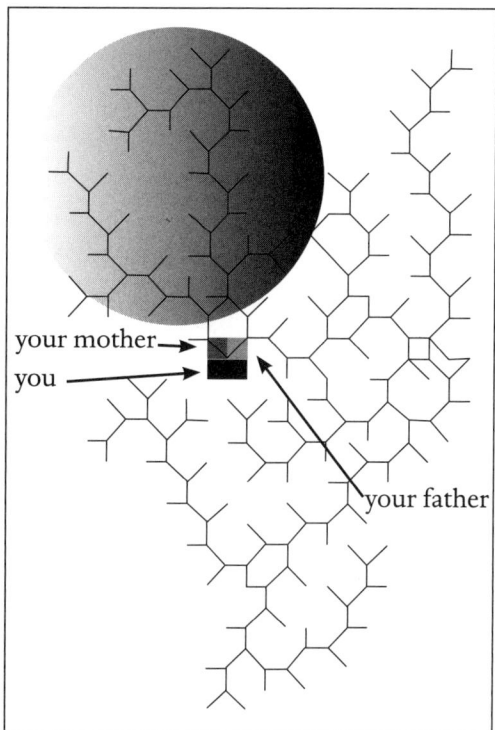

Figure 1

Now the interesting mathematics:

If you had two parents and they had two parents, their pair of parents would make four people. If these four parents each had a pair of parents, that would make eight people. So if these eight people also had a pair of parents, we have sixteen—and so on. Suggesting an average generation as being twenty-five years, can you calculate how many direct parental ancestors you have had in the last two thousand years? Multiply that figure by five hundred and forty million years.

How then can anyone ever predict the future, either for an individual or a nation? And how can anyone hold these events to any biologically-recognized lifespan?

It's mind-boggling. The only explanation that makes sense is that the events have already occurred in one way or another.

How do I justify this? The universe is still catching up with itself.

Again considering the big bang, we are informed that in a matter of a speculative 10^{43} of a second, energy expanded throughout the known universe in an almost equal, yet asymmetrical quantity of matter and antimatter. As these two materials were created they collided—destroying each other—creating pure energy. It took another infinitely small period of time for common particles to form. These particles are called baryons, and include photons, neutrinos, electrons, and quarks that would become the building blocks of matter and life as we know it. During the baryon genesis period there were no recognizable heavy particles such as protons or neutrons because of the intense heat—it was merely quark soup. As the universe began to cool and expand even more, we begin to understand more clearly what exactly happened.

Within two to three minutes the universe had cooled to about 3000 billion degrees Kelvin[4] and, to cut a very long story short, matter began its journey to becoming matter, expanding forever outward from its hypothesized source.

The point here is that matter *follows* energy and not only that, they co-exist, knowing each other, at the same time.

---

[4] In 1933, the International Committee of Weights and Measures adopted the triple point of water—the temperature at which water, ice, and water vapor coexist in equilibrium—as the Kelvin.

The Chicken or the Egg—Collapsing the Wave

I read Darryl Reanney's first book, *The Death of Forever* (Longman, Australia, 1991), not long after its publication, and it changed the way I think of time, reality, and matter.

I started exploring for correlations between Quantum thought, mysticism, and Tarot, and they are obvious—the ramifications startling.

What if the events predicted through the Tarot would never have occurred if they had not been predicted?

I admit that the thought had been around for a long time. I'd asked my grandmother—who read cards and tea leaves, and who could predict times and names and places—how it all worked. She was the first person to raise the conundrum of the "chicken or the egg"—the possibility that Tarot actually, in some inexplicable way, causes the events that it predicts. For over two decades I refused to consider the possibility (definite denial) because the responsibility then becomes somewhat uncomfortable.

If this is the case, then how does it happen?

I am aware of several things…

Light and Thought

The mind and the brain are not necessarily the same thing. The mind is an aware thing; it contains all our knowledge in our lives thus far; it is the mansion of the imagination; it is a vessel for symbol, allegory, all our value judgments, our learned or programmed reactions to external events, information. The mind seems to reside in our heads—in our brains—but is that necessarily so? Couldn't it as easily be that mind (us without the body) does not exist in time at all; does not exist within the parameters of perceived reality; is interpreted *within* the brain just as all external stimuli is interpreted? For the sake of this book I'm going to make a not-so-implausible jump and say that mind and soul are the *same,* so that throughout the work I can jump from the one word to the other with impunity.

So what does the brain do? It's marvelous, really—it interprets everything we sense and think into response-and-react mode, sorts and categorizes—all while telling the body what to do in a million, million unrecognized, unconscious ways. It is like some Into-the-Future computer beyond our current wildest dreams as neural pathways and synapses explode and transmit and interpret absolutely everything.

Thought is something that everyone does most of the time and there are several different kinds of thought. The following three images are to be understood thus:

- The central line is the line between outer and inner self.
- The wave that moves over this central line is thought.
- The grey-matter is accumulated knowledge and other mind-based material.
- The strangely panoramic, mountainous place at the base of the images is Elsewhere—the places we can visit beyond the realms of what we perceive as manifest reality and where, also, things or entities other than those with which we are familiar in manifest reality can also connect with us.

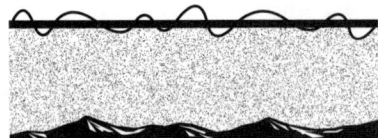

Figure 2: Surface Chatter

a. This represents surface chatter and thought-in-continuum. This is like white-noise—we are aware of it sometimes and sometimes it is completely unconscious. This aspect of thought can flit through our consciousness by way of colorful scenes, snippets of conversation, passing memories of things we have done, and plans and schedules yet to occur. There are any number of variations—unremembered and seemingly inconsequential to whatever task we are currently undertaking.

b. The second aspect of thought I would ask you to consider is when we trap a passing thought and follow it. When this function occurs, we temporarily block out unrelated information. That does not mean that surface chatter is

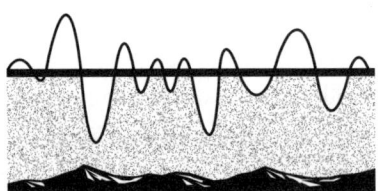

Figure 3: Conscious Thinking

no longer happening—because it is—but it becomes the less dominant experience. When conscious thinking is invoked we are prioritizing; we are bringing mind into the equation. This happens during study of any kind, when concentrated activity is undertaken, or when our attention cannot or does not allow for distraction. Note how the line remains in this image and that the spikes below the line are not filled. This is meant to convey the understanding that we are also aware of our surroundings and external undertakings and events simultaneous to the deep-thought process.

Let's say I want to understand the nature of time. I would have been led to this desire by any of an incalculable number of snippets and bits of information over the years, some of which have irked me: *You never have any time for me; I've run out of time; I've got time to kill; don't waste time;* even *Once upon a time*—expressions that commodify that which is beyond commodification.

The contemplation will take on all the recognized and random qualities of what I have learned throughout my life including the ability to prophesy events that supposedly do not exist yet, and I will, in some mystifying way, have them all swirling around in me as I seek a doorway through the seconds, minutes, years, and eons that we—as a species—have created.

c. The third aspect is deep, deep contemplation and meditation. This occurs through an act of intention, and it breaches the so-called boundaries of thought, becoming something quite mystical, and when we have reached this place—once our line of reality ceases to pose a consensual limitation—our daily consciousness allows for constant connection.

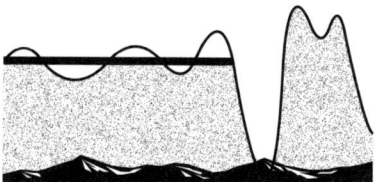

Figure 4: Breaching the Boundaries

This can (sometimes) generate an even deeper response—beyond thought—where something not in mind beforehand reaches out to meet us from beyond the confines of personal process.

This is deep thought, where you go so deeply into the abyss of mind that an unseen, inexplicable membrane—one that *seems* to separate self from something absolutely vast—can give us access to other intelligences, deities, spirits, mysteries, inspirations, and utter epiphanies that will irrevocably alter the way we understand life.

Like light, thought is in a seeming *wave* state, because the thing about thought is that it isn't anywhere and, like light, it can exhibit itself as both wave and particle. What transforms thought into particle? Contact.

Whether thoughts and ideas manifest in a material outcome depends on our transmission of them into perceived reality. Unit 3 deals with alternate realities but it is necessary to mention (while I think of it) that the future does not, in any true sense, exist. Not until events happen, and are recognized as happening, does the so-called future come into being, and by the time it does the events will have *already occurred*—therefore the events are already in the so-called past.

There is, as was mentioned earlier, no beginning to anything and no end either, and all such considerations are value judgments, very human and open to error (in the light of future history) because—as modern physics clearly demonstrates—there is no such thing as an impartial observation.

A person coming to your table to have their Tarot read—to have you predict their future for them—will do so for many reasons, but all of them are serious.

Some of those reasons are—

- They may come as a seeming outright skeptic. I wonder why someone would pay good money to satisfy themselves that the psychic is a fraud. It does not compute. They may very well even *want* you to be a fraud! That would provide them with a sense of safety that the real deal would disrupt unimaginably.
- They will come out of mere curiosity because someone else came before them and perhaps talked them into it.
- They will come for you to tell them that everything in their screwed-up lives will work out okay.

- They will come to have you give them answers to their choices.
- Some will come for the sheer privacy and company that only a total stranger can provide.
- If you have a reputation for accuracy they will come because they want to hear what you have to say.

The bottom line is that they were always going to come because they *did* come.

Could they have avoided coming? No, because they have already been to see you and along the way to seeing you were countless alternatives and none were taken.

The thing about the chicken and the egg is that it cuts both ways.

So what happens?

The client makes the initial contact. That has changed both of your realities. Even the so-called skeptic's reality has changed—they have made contact with the enemy. An appointment is made within time as we know it and therefore, somewhere unseen, a chain reaction is occurring and will continue to occur forever. It is only within the tiniest window of each of our lives that something that utterly defies the laws of probability happens.

Let me describe the central theme of the interpretation:

- The client arrives and is ushered into the private space of the reader.
- The reader, after whatever procedure they use to prepare the cards, hands them to the client.
- The client shuffles the deck of seventy-eight cards illustrated with images and symbols and hands them back to the reader, who lays them face up on the table in certain pre-learned patterns, and begins to talk.
- The reader continues to do all the talking until that section of the reading is completed, at which time the client is asked for their specific questions.
- When the procedure is completed the client pays the agreed sum and departs.

Sounds simple enough?

It isn't.

Everything plays a part in what happens next: the client; their DNA interacting with the paper of a series of images that have inherent meaning, albeit in symbol-form; and the interpretation of that set of symbols in a pre-learned pattern that basically tells a series of stories and events, complete with emotion and sensation.

The thing is . . . when you begin to speak you are collapsing what was, until that moment, the probability of only one of very many possible futures! You have entered into the perceived world a material essence—your voice. You have imprinted your words into the mind of the client. *What is spoken cannot be unspoken.*

There are two things to understand:

- Much of a reading could be forgotten if not recorded.
- Readings that are recorded are material realities (as much as any recorded sound can be).

Matter is slower than light, therefore material events will unfold more slowly than the thought or spoken word because matter has to catch up. But it will—no matter how bizarre the reading, no matter how out of left field.

Examples will be given in the units on case histories and the more traditional and mystical explanation will be given in the units on Tarot and the Tree of Life.

Oh, and my first meeting with Time as a god? That was back in 1990 (on the Gregorian calendar) during a specific series of rituals over a ten-week period.

Raziel

(I am seated at my altar. The candles are lit. My Grimoir is open, my pen resting unused upon the pages, and I am deep in meditation.)

I heard—

"Good morning."

"??? Good morning?" (I don't yet know what's going on; in the vision of the meditation I'm on a rock, outside a small cave, in a cove of beach before dawn. I can open my eyes and have my consciousness remain in the two places, temple and beach, while I write down what I've just heard.)

He says, "Have you time?"

"I have time."

"Must you write everything down as we speak?"

"I would forget it otherwise."

"Very well, let me dream with you . . . Look upon the waters of the world. See the sparkling silver light? The silver dawn? A boulder is there upon which to sit before my cave where I lay waiting."

The landscape is pre-dawn; pale grey sea; pale grey sky; narrow beach, boulder-strewn; caves and high cliffs all around the sand.

"Can I ask you something?"

"We are at peace, we can speak."

"You said that you were waiting in there," I said, looking toward the cave behind us, "...waiting for what?"

"For time."

"What do you mean?"

"Death takes place within and without, you know."

"Are you dead?"

"Wait, sit a moment . . ." *I see him then, although vaguely—he reminds me of a Merlin-type person.*

"Look! Look at the rabbits."

There, up along the sand, by the water's edge, are hundreds of them.

"They play, you know."

"I don't understand any of this . . . Are you dead?"

"Oh, don't be so trivial!"

"You said you were waiting."

"Look, I haven't much time to speak to you, so listen, look, and feel with me."

He took my hands and looked into my eyes and said, "Do I look very old to you?"

"Yes."

"But I haven't got a face, you know."

"You show me one."

He laughs. "Oh, the images we choose to see!"

"What are you then?"

He ignored my question, "Oh, I'm tired of looking old."

"What are you waiting for?"

"Oh, a time when spring is young and fresh and no one tries to take the stage."

"What do you mean?"

"Oh, everyone forgets about me."

"Then who are you?"

"I am time!"

"I don't understand."

"You will if you remember me with love. I cherish every moment of my life with you and would have it last eternally—but you will go a-racing with tomorrow; they always do. And I am left haunted by my memories . . . Before I look to hold them near they are gone, oh fleet-of-foot."

"What are you waiting for?"

"Oh, just a little ball of someone's time to stay and play with me."

"You said you were within the cave?"

"The memory of me dwells there, yes, but I am here with you just once; the memory will last a thousand lifetimes."

"It isn't just me you're talking to, is it?"

"You're the only one here."

"How long would you like me to stay?"

"You just did!"

"Can I come again?"

"I won't be here anymore."

"I don't understand."

"Oh, well, we wait, then, you and I."

After a long pause I ask, "Why can't I come again?"

"I will have changed by then."

"Into what?"

"Yesterday!" . . . Penguins, now, and sea-birds and wild, wild winds of winter wash the many waves away and grains of sand are left for me to play with.

"You seem so lonely."

"No! I have never been lonely. There are so many of me you couldn't count me by all the stars in space."

I have already mentioned that he was a Merlin-like presence which accounts for the next comment.

"You lost me, Merlin."

"What did you call me?"

"Sorry, that was presumptuous . . . I got my myths mixed up."

He roared laughing; rolled around and around on the sand.

"It'll do, it'll do! You made me laugh—here, I have a gift for you . . ."

And he pointed out over the sea, all grey and silver with pre-dawn light. As I watched the sun began to burnish the horizon with its gold.

"Life! Isn't it a miracle! And no one seems to know how much a passion it is."

"I have to go."

"You always did."

"I don't want to feel guilty about going."

"What? And waste time? No."

And he took my face in his hands and said—

"Cherish me, and take the morning as my gift."

UNIT TWO

What Tarot Is and What It Isn't

Minimalist History

What Tarot *isn't*, is just a pack of seventy-eight cards. It's way bigger and much more exciting.

I'd like to remind you about the soup of one-celled creatures floating in the viscous seas of infant Earth with no discernible differences to blowflies or elephants mentioned in Unit 1. What applies to us as a species and to our immortality also applies to the entirety of everything including these seventy-eight cards that in the not-so-distant past were blowing in the wind of some forest somewhere, the outcome of every seed that preceded it, and so on. So it is with everything, and there is absolutely *no such thing* as an inanimate object.

The word *Tarot* is French. In Italy it was/is known as *Tarocchi* from the earlier *Carte da Trionfi* (or cards of triumph), in Germany as *Tarock*, in Hungary *Tarokk*. It's suspected that the word originated in the Arabic *Taraha* (reject) but no one knows for sure. There's power in words, but it seems to me that the power invested in the word stems from what the cards actually do . . .

Individually they do NOTHING!

Tarot is a word to describe a technique of prophecy that works. It is able to predict events that have seemingly not yet occurred, moreso than any other technique, even down to exact times, names, places, and descriptions.

Tarot is not a tool of comfort, advice, past-life analysis, or spiritual/emotional/psychological analysis—it will only ever tell the client what they will experience or know, no matter *what* the client *wants* you to tell them. It is blunt and as often disturbing as it is reassuring, and . . . it can interrupt personal readings with other pertinent information such as world events or even the stories of other people that the client has not even met and may never meet, but will assuredly know of.

Tarot will teach you, if it trusts you to continue learning, because Tarot *is* Time. It is Him/Her/Us/Them/It—and none of these—because all of these are objectifications. And it knows what is to come. It will only trust you if you remain flexible and unattached to what you say, and it will only trust you if you *tell* what you see, no matter how seemingly stupid, off-the-wall, crazy, uncomfortable, or unbelievable it might seem to either you or the client!

Reading Tarot is like becoming a computer-priest: technician, software creator, consultant, and hacker; understanding symbols and utilizing every bit of possible data that is available in both the world as we know it *and* the world we may not yet recognize or understand (and I am not even beginning to discuss other worlds).

Practice: The Personal Energetic Field and Body Language

For Tarot cards to behave as a medium through which prophecy travels, it is necessary to have both a transmitter and a receiver: the client and the interpreter. In this manner a third force is activated—utterly unknown and, as yet, unknowable—therefore occult.

I realize that there is quite a trend in *distance* or phone readings, but I am unaware, personally, of whether they are valid. I do not use this function because I know what works for me and that is field-to-field contact.

You can practice understanding personal energetic fields through what the human body itself informs in many differing circumstances. It's more interesting to do so by way of observation before you ask your friends to assist you.

Over a typical week, observe people in any group of three or more.

Observe, first, who is the most dominant person in the group, and ascertain the amount of space between each person present. Nine times out of ten the other members of the group will maintain an equidistant space from each other. It is very obvious when seated around a dining table—how uncomfortable can you cause another individual to feel if you move only 20 centimeters closer to them?

Intimidation almost always relies on entering another's personal space, whereas dislike, distrust, or initial meetings will be the opposite until one or the other offers the hand of friendship, effectively closing the gap.

Before discussing energy fields with my students, I ask them to stand in a circle without explaining why. When they are settled in place, I go around the circle and measure the space between each body, and always, without exception, there is the exact same distance between each person. This indicates where their relative fields (commonly called auras) connect.

You can set these scenarios up yourself and observe the distance between people under differing circumstances.

It is advisable to record your findings in your journal for future reference if teaching these techniques to others.

This transaction of relative energy always occurs between client and reader. You enter into their field—you *merge*. Successful prophecy occurs when the reader is basically possessed by the client!

This is why, in most cases, self-prophecy does not work because of zero objectivity and nothing to bounce off, and why, when training, it is advisable to work with others.

UNIT THREE

Who Defines 'Reality'?

Theory: Shadow Reality/Multiple Reality and Alternative Lives

So what came first? Were events predicted by Tarot already in existence somewhere? What constitutes the theory of predestination? Is there such a thing as free will? Can we change the future or are we doomed (or blessed) to play out preset parameters like some production written in the hand of some insane god? *What* does the predicting anyway?

The answers to questions one and two are covered in Unit 1 to a degree, and all of the considerations I am going to present are theories—some backed up by secret personal polls I have conducted over the years, hopefully worthy of your consideration.

Having established the possibility that the soul/mind both inhabits us as a body, and does not, where else (and what else) could it be, and what could it be doing?

Multiple Lives: Ourselves in the Future, Our Connection with Many Gods—Close Encounters of the Second Kind

As a witch I was called to the priesthood of my Craft before I was twelve years old and it was just that—a Calling; a communication that bypassed my ears, going straight to my brain[1]. This occurred, along with an entire year of odd psychic encounters, a couple of near-death experiences, the winning of my first national essay competition, and one of those dreams that influences your entire life, so that, by the time I was thirteen, I was holding séances for the public, feeling weirdly religious, and becoming extremely interested in boys.

By the time I was sixteen, I was an outrageous rebel who also happened to be a member of Sydney's only Psychic Research Society, during the enlightened '60s when parapsychology was becoming acceptable in many universities throughout the world and the Eastern bloc was investing extensive time, academics, and money in the study of the so-called paranormal.

By my late seventeenth year I was an initiated witch and was reading Tarot (not very well, retrospectively).

Throughout there was that unseen voice assisting me to explore pertinent books, warning me about boys, and talking no-nonsense at me when life became overwhelming.

The voice was sometimes a she and sometimes a he, but never was I given any names. My understanding of different pantheons of gods and goddesses came about through study and communication with like-minded others.

I am clairaudient.

Over the years there have been many of these encounters, often with different gods and goddesses, daemons, elementals, and entities, and each was so dominant when present—teaching me so much—that I always felt they were with me for the long run, but they never were. They came and went as the seasons of change demanded, as circumstances decreed.

Sometimes I am given names to know them by and other times I am not, but Tarot has been with me for over three decades.

The god of Tarot is Time and he tends to think the whole human relationship to him is hilarious, or sad, depending on the circumstances.

---

1 Within the cerebral hemispheres of the brain are the temporal lobes, which nest under the parietal and frontal lobes. Whether you appreciate birdsong or rock music, your brain responds through the activity of these lobes. At the top of each temporal lobe is an area responsible for receiving information from the ears, while other parts of this lobe seem to integrate memories and sensations of taste, sound, sight, and touch.

Time, as a god, is eternal, immortal, non-linear, larger than space, older than our concept of the theory of the big bang, and infinitely open to humor and communication.

Then comes that funny feeling again: that perhaps the voice that has guided my life (and it *is* a woman's voice) is me! Maybe from the future; maybe as the axis of *Infinity's Web*, who knows? What tweaked that line of thinking were two conversations: one with my long-time friend Bernard Casimir, and the other with a young Druid scholar and musician that I have known for several years. Both had dreams of old men instructing them regarding their present. Both described the old men but couldn't see the correlation that was obvious within the descriptions: that the men they described sounded remarkably like much older versions of themselves.

None of this is far-fetched when we consider modern technological advances. I remember sitting in front of the TV a very long time ago, wondering how it was possible that a live commentary could be transferred through the airwaves interpreting itself into image, movement, and sound—pixels trapped in a miniature box.

You can spend your entire life in awe at the idea of information bouncing in waves from a satellite orbiting the earth, at the knowledge that yellow dirt mined in outback Australia is responsible for the creation of nuclear weapons and technology.

Being in communication with unseen intelligences is such an ancient thing—an ancient mysticism—and it can be dismissed as irrational or loopy by contemporary reductionism and ultra-rationalist, pre-quantum thought . . . but that's simply untrue. What it is, is Fate.

To Die, or Not to Die, That Is the Question

The curious question of what constitutes death is always open to speculation. On one hand, due to the thorough research that has gone into NDEs (Near-Death Experiences), we have countless credible records of out-of-body experiences. On the other hand there is what Tarot has taught me:

I don't recall the exact year, but it was while I was still living in Victoria, over twenty years ago, when I had my first AIDS client. I recall vividly seeing this man's first spread of the reading and the impact. All I saw was the current television warning regarding the virus, and I sat unmoving, not certain how to proceed.

"Tell me everything," he said.

I took a deep breath and said, "I see the Grim Reaper ad on the telly."

"I've got full-blown AIDS," he proceeded to inform me. "I just want to know how long I've got so I can be ready."

I will love that man forever for letting me off the hook so quickly and easily with what I saw and for helping me to learn what I did, and Tarot, for what happened next. Over several months it sent me AIDS sufferer after AIDS sufferer. I read for hundreds, and the only time I saw actual death *was always for someone else*! Loved ones, friends, colleagues. The experience of death was in the observation of it happening elsewhere. In each of these boys' readings (many whom, over time, I was told had died) the 10 of Cups presented itself as the outcome!

The bottom-line interpretation of that card is HOME.

That doesn't mean that whenever that card comes up, as a consistent outcome throughout the many spreads you will do, that the client will die—far from it—because many other factors have to be recognized for this to be the case, but why would Tarot keep repeating the same outcome?

To teach me something I needed to understand (I have had many such learning times, but more on that later), I needed to understand the image of hopscotch! (figure 5, below)

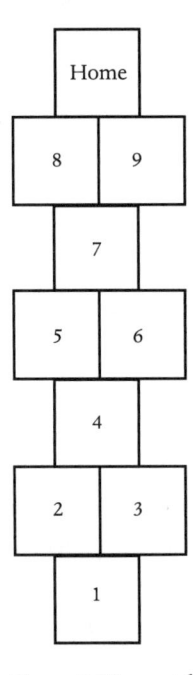

Figure 5: Hopscotch

Hopscotch is thought to have originated in ancient Britain during the early incursions of the Romans. The original hopscotch courts were over 100 feet long and used for military training exercises where Roman foot soldiers ran the course in full armor and field packs to improve their footwork, much in the way modern footballers train, or the military sets up obstacle courses for trainee soldiers.

Children drew their own smaller courts in imitation of the soldiers and added a scoring system. The word "London" is often written at the top of a hopscotch court, reminiscent of the Great North Road: a four-hundred-mile-long Roman road that ran from Glasgow to London, frequently used by the Roman military.

Conclusion? It is like life—a seeming obstacle course, dependent sometimes on skill, sometimes on seeming fate, to get the participant to Home where they are safe and have completed the game.

What I found interesting and inspirational is that I use the Tree of Life spread during a client consultation, whereby Kether is both the outcome and the most profound achievement of the spread (figure 6). Note the similarity to the hopscotch game:

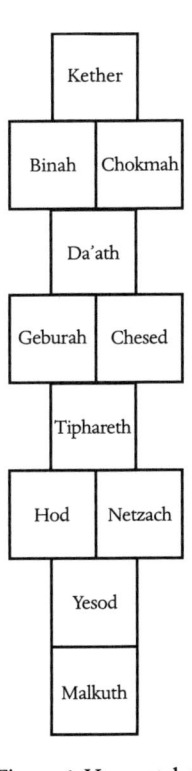

Figure 6: Hopscotch 2

What Tarot was teaching was that death is not part of the personally experiential equation!

With this in mind I introduced into my classes a visualization exercise. Each student closes their eyes and imagines a little blue man with green hair and tentacles instead of ears, dressed like a children's book image of a pixie with spectacles perched on the tip of his nose, holding a candle in one hand and an open book in the other, from which he appears to be reading intently.

Everyone nods—yes, they can see him.

I then ask the class to close their eyes and imagine being dead. None could do so. They could imagine seeing themselves in a coffin. Some imagined space, some imagined being elsewhere as either themselves or other people, some imagined seeing their dead bodies laid out for burial—but not the experience of being dead.

This could, of course, be a deeply-rooted denial. It could also be that there is absolutely no knowledge of when the bodily functions cease.

Because of some very interesting events that happened to both me and others close to me, I asked thousands of the people I met, over several years: "Have you ever had a life-threatening illness or accident, or a near-death experience?"

Of those who answered "Yes," I asked what had occurred in their lives afterward. Most of these people had undergone big shifts. Many moved home, changed their relationships, jobs, way of living, way of viewing life—there were endless variations.

What if they had actually died? What if all the recognized changes that occurred post-trauma were because they had awoken in another of their bodies with mere variations to the one that ceased?

In *Witchcraft: Theory and Practice* (Llewellyn, USA, 2000), I wrote the following in the chapter *Dreamwalker* (p. 168):

- *There are those powerful dreams whereby you leave the landscape of recognizable reality and voyage, through the dreamweb, to other worlds wherein you also live, retaining the memory of experiences upon waking into your current recognizable reality.*
- *Then there are the times when you'll meet with gods or beings from the landscape of magic; the times when you'll be in the company of people you know from the past, present, or future.*

And I gave an example of the taped reading of a woman who died where several post-death experiences were recorded.

There are several other post-death experiences on the same tape.

Contemplation of all this raised a theory of parallel lives; as though we experience lives like outward-facing multifacets on a sphere—recognition of each being only realized at the centre—one life being experienced multifariously. Another symbol of parallel lives being an infinitely mirrored kaleidoscope, the whole-self being the pieces that are not mirrored, knowing themselves through their refraction.

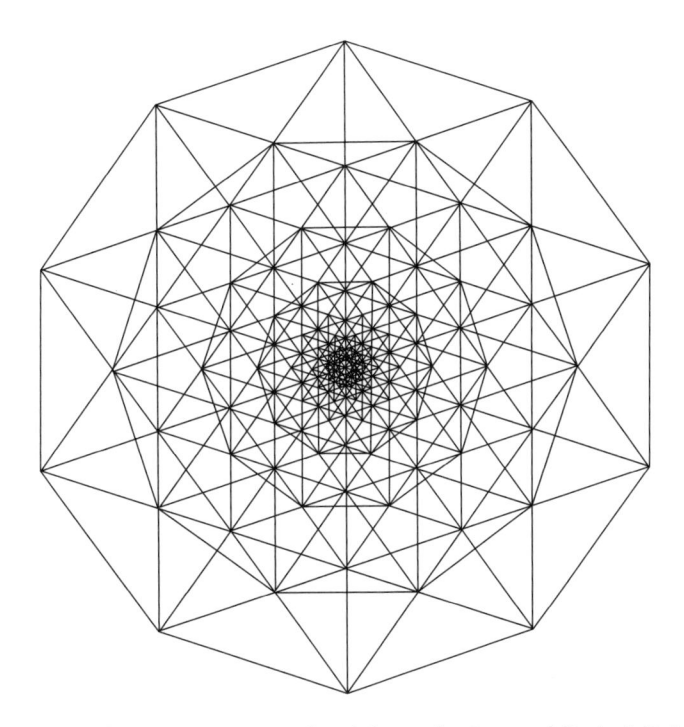

Figure 7: Infinity (*Infinity's Web*—hand-drawn by Bernard Casimir B.A.)

The above diagram (figure 7) gives an idea of what "*. . . theory of parallel lives; as though we experience lives like outward-facing multifacets on a sphere. . .*" would look like as a model, each outward-facing facet representing what you are experiencing as you are within your life today. But you are simultaneously every other facet facing outward, experiencing a view of life, unable to see your neighboring lives by the mere fact of facing out.

If we take the theory one step further and declare the model *organic,* we could almost say that each life that ceases is like sloughing off dead skin cells, rejuvenating that which is exposed; or that each life is seasonal and dies when it is its time; when it ceases to be productive to the remaining facets of self who grow and are stimulated by the nourishment provided by one's own decomposing fruit.

If we then take the dive into a not-so-improbable immortality, the concept of both past lives and an afterlife take on a whole new perspective and congruity, therefore any one of you can actually turn up in a reading, even though it is rare.

What is *not* rare is the so-called dead being present at a reading. I often have a difficult time explaining to the client that the individual is actually not dead in the way they think of it.

Four Distinct Case Histories

Sometimes (not often) the Death card actually means just that, but always as a consideration rather than an event; in other instances, when the event is yet to occur, it will show itself as a pattern of a minimum of two cards.

The Woman from the Adelaide Hills

The crowning card in the present of this woman's Celtic Cross was the Death card, so the first thing I was aware of was that death, or endings, was having an immediate affect on this person's life. As the reading progressed, and among other things that are gone from memory, I had a great deal to say about the man who loves her in her future, giving description and detail of his appearance, his habits, his pleasures, etc.

I concluded—with the Key (three cards chosen at random)—that even though the man described throughout the reading loves her utterly, he is unable to tell her (2 of Swords).

When it came time for her to ask me any questions she just sat stunned.

The man I had described as being her partner in the future had been buried the month before she came to see me.

He continues to live with her, you see? For him, nothing has changed. Tarot does not relate to him as having gone anywhere!

Who Buried Who?

The second example occurred within a week of the last. A young woman came to see me and again, in the first spread: Celtic Cross, the Death card was the crowning card.

Yadayada, on I chat, until the question section when she asks me to tell her about her father. I lay out the spread and burst into tears because I am so sad for him. He has just buried his daughter and is bereft.

She buried *him* the week before coming to see me. That's not his experience—for him it's the other way around.

The Woman in the Bell Jar

This was initially tricky. For the first two spreads I went on about the client's alcohol problem, her futile life, that she wasn't a natural mother and resented her children, and that her relationship with her husband was an abominable mess.

She was horrified.

"That's not me!" she exclaimed. "You've got it all wrong!"

I suggested she could choose to allow me to continue, or she could choose to leave. She agreed to continue, despite the confusion.

In the following spread I saw the distinct image of the battered and bloody body of a woman in a large glass bell jar, her face forced up against the side, an eye open and pleading. It was not my client. What was I to say? What I saw.

The client became very disturbed as she realized what was happening.

Her sister had been dead for three years. She had been an alcoholic with a history of disturbing behavior and domestic upheaval. She had wandered off one night in her pajamas and dressing gown and her body—what was left of it—had been found in daylight. She had wandered onto a freeway in Sydney and had been run down.

The client had been to a psychic in Sydney some time later who had told her that her sister was at peace and had "gone to the light."

Unfortunately that was not true. According to Tarot she was still there and I suggested the client go to the site and yell out to her sister that she is dead so that she knew.

The Hanged Man

I had a client come up to me in the street and remind me of his reading. Twelve months or so beforehand I had informed him that there would be the death of a young man in the family, that this would be enormously distressing for all concerned, mainly due to a lack of information regarding the death itself. Tarot told him to tell the people that the death was this man's destiny, that no one was to blame, and that they should respect his right to have chosen this option because—for him—there had been no alternative, and that he loves them all deeply.

My client's cousin (his mother's sister's son) was twenty-eight years old and hung himself, leaving no note or any kind of explanation whatsoever. My client took the tape to the family in Western Australia and played it for them.

They still grieved, but because of what was on the tape—over a year prior to the death—they found some sense of peace.

So if death is not the end—if more than any consideration of what we believe life to be is occurring parallel or unrecognized by us—why aren't we aware of this? My first thought is *overload*, and my second thought is that we *are* aware but we do not allow ourselves to consciously know it so that we are constantly surprised by experience . . . and, after all, it is for experience that we live.

What about other worlds, other dimensions, other so-called time frames?

It depends on what is meant by other worlds. Are we talking about other planets? Other galaxies? Does it matter? To Tarot it's all *this* world. It's all now (no matter when 'now' is), and it can and will teach it all, and *not* simply when you are working with the cards. The thing about Tarot is that when you *become* Tarot it will work with you whenever you are open to it, which is whenever you don't need your attention on the steering wheel of your car as you navigate heavy traffic in an unknown city.

Shadow Reality

Shadow lives also exist. Every time life presents you with a choice, and you decide to go one way over another, a shadow reality occurs because what you didn't choose continues its influence.

What that actually means is that although you have only one single destiny there are a plethora of ways that that destiny can express itself. The very fact that you have made the choices that you have made throughout your life informs you that you are fulfilling your destiny, and that it is the sum of your decisions and choices thus far that reinforce your destiny as perfect. Value judgments placed on the seeming importance of one person's destiny over another's are sheer arrogance and garbage. If something was not destined to happen it would not have happened—that which has already occurred *could not have been avoided because it has happened.*

The beauty of experience is that there are no mistakes; there are only building blocks for other experiences, which is why I tell people who are embarrassed at fumbling with cards or having difficulty shuffling, that it doesn't matter because they cannot make a mistake. This is also why I suggest that people who are dissatisfied with their lives take calculated risks—after all, we all eventually die, don't we? And it's all natural because, as mentioned earlier, it is not possible to be separated from life, only to express our uniqueness in the matter of how we live it.

Back to shadow reality.

Tarot will sometimes raise an analogy. It may seem to discuss another person's past or present (not as in the case of the woman in the bell jar) like a metaphor that doesn't, initially, make sense to the client. Most often the client will have their bells go off after the reading and will phone me with the realization at some later stage, after having listened to the tape of the session one or more times.

Case History

I recall doing a reading for a quite famous witch. In the spread called *Other People and Specific Events*—two lines of cards with a foundation card at the bottom—where Tarot discusses other people who do, or will, have a direct bearing on our lives in the future, two distinctly different women were mentioned: one on the top line, one on the bottom, with the Queen that represented the client as the significator[2]—the foundation card.

The woman on the top line was married, with children, but her life was one of seemingly perpetual inconsequence, whereas the woman on the second line was obviously a veiled member of an orthodox religion—she looked like a nun—in constant conflict with the rigidity of the establishment.

There seemed no relevance at the time, but when this woman later listened to the tape, she remembered. She was brought up a Roman Catholic and in the heat of prepubescent zeal she had decided she wanted to be a nun, not realizing at that stage that the calling she was experiencing was of a much more pagan persuasion, because we cannot know that for which we have no reference until it is discovered mirrored in the world around us. She had also married in her early twenties and had children, but the marriage demanded that she give away the whimsy of Witchcraft and be a *normal* woman . . . and she had almost allowed family coercion to win over her natural inclinations, until she'd realized that the

---

2 The significator is the card used to represent the person having the reading.

option was untenable, and she had gone through the rigors of divorce for the sake of her sanity, rather than acquiesce to the alternative.

What Tarot had shown her were her shadow realities, and it had shown her those for a reason. That woman went on to read Tarot herself, understanding that she *must* know, intimately, as many variations of experience as possible to be able to enter into the zone of another person. That was what Tarot taught her from that spread.

We are not alive to become rich or famous or safe or beautiful or talented—we are alive to live life with the intention of doing it very well. We cannot do that without experience.

Those shadow realities will be playing themselves out as one of the other facets on the example of *Infinity's Web* and, as in the case of the other witch just mentioned, with an increased yearning to experience more, or other, than what she has chosen (either that or one or both of the women in that spread died at the point of choice) because the knowledge and awareness of one of the 'selves' passes on to all others.

Free Will and Fate

Do we create our future as we go along? Can we, through an act of intention, set up future events that we walk into?

The answer is yes. And no.

For many years I didn't think this way—not in regard to fate[3] in general—but I have learned that we underestimate life by thinking that it's already set when at any given moment, because of any choice or decision we make, it will and does change.

The first thing to realize is that no one is here for a purpose as though by divine right and I raise that topic because at least one in ten people will ask you to ask Tarot "What is my purpose?" Each person makes their own through intention and circumstance; through action. To all of these people I say the answer is to live their lives exquisitely, no matter how grand or how simple, and to experiment whenever possible; to take risks if necessary and to trust that some things are certain (like body-death) but, as was said earlier, that may not necessarily be what we have been conditioned to believe it to be.

---

3 Fate—from L. *fata*, neut. pl. of *fatum* "thing spoken (by the gods), one's destiny," from neut. pp. of *fari* "to speak." The L. sense evolution is from "sentence of the Gods" (Gk. theosphaton), subsequently "lot, portion" (Gk. moira, personified as a goddess in Homer), later "one of the three goddesses (Clotho, Lachesis, and Atropos) who determined the course of a human life."

Through clear intention it is possible to set up events in the future through actions in the present, as long as we remain patient, because often mountains must be moved for those events to unfold. It's very much spell-crafting, so it's necessary to be careful with what we set up because if a specific pattern of destiny is already in motion then chaos is what it will take to realign that pattern.

When I read Tarot (and bear in mind it was the client's unavoidable destiny to have their cards read by virtue of their being read) I always inform the client of what Tarot does:

The events that Tarot predicts will happen. What you do about those events is where free will comes in. Each event is like a doorway clearly marked. The outcome of the event is rarely given because not only your actions and intentions but those of others will come into play once the event is realized. The only absolutes are birth and death, and even then there is an after.

People often ask me how long before they can come again and my usual answer is "When the events have happened, or sufficient numbers of them to open doors to other probabilities." This is most important because:

1. There are Tarot junkies.
2. Whenever a follow-up reading occurs, Tarot is often disinclined to mention the events that have not happened, and can often make events seem larger than they will be because of the time factor. By this I mean that events that have been predicted over an approximate two-year period will be magnified in a shorter time span, so that financial wealth (Sun card, Ace of Wands) within the span of two years could represent thousands and thousands of dollars, but if the client comes back in six months with none of the events having yet happened, the same two cards could represent finding a $50 note on the street.
3. You, as the reader, will lose your objectivity if you read for the same person too many times, as it is necessary to forget almost everything that you read until (and if) you are reminded at some later stage (it's called "having a life of your own"), and that forgetting is imperative because you may very well have family or friends of theirs referred to you and you must work on a clean slate with each person, seemingly knowing nothing about them.

The Random Factor

Accurate prediction of events that are recognized explicitly in the light of the future cannot be a random thing, but there *are* oddball things that happen and often these are hidden by The Fool card.

Whenever The Fool card shows up without the interaction of other cards it hides an event that the client is not to know about. It does this because some things have to seem like accidents if they are to change the client's future. This is a paradox because:

1. The client would most certainly have set up this accident as a means of changing a problem situation in their life, and
2. They are afraid to change the problem thing in their life and therefore require the intervention of the random element or fate to trigger the job for them.

The only other random thing that I'm aware of shows up in my Warning Spread, which I fondly also call the Stupid Spread, because it will show an event that can be utterly avoided because it will be seen coming, and the client would have to be naïve or stupid to buy into it if they've seen it coming.

Part Two
Tarot, the Living Tradition

UNIT FOUR

Communication and Perception

Practice: Communication vs. Babble

Either discuss with your group, or write in your journal, the difference between *communication* and *babble*. Spend time observing others and talking with them without entering any excess words into the conversation. If they talk babble ask them to explain what they really mean.

Get people talking about themselves, their experiences, and viewpoints.

Watch their body language and understand what they are saying *without* words.

Be aware of both your emotional and your physical reactions and responses to what is said, and whether you are being sufficiently open to reading them on many levels. If you intuitively pick up passing thought scraps that seem to be precognitive, either pass the information, casually and worded respectfully and carefully, on to the person concerned or keep a note of it in your journal.

An example of the above is if Mary phones you and tells you she is getting married to John and the small voice in your mind whispers, *"Oh-oh!"* I wouldn't say anything, of course, but I would certainly file the thought away for future reference. The same thing could be if a friend informs you she is pregnant and without any searching the small inner voice says, *"It's a girl."*

The more you take note of this inner voice, the more it will communicate with you. You may actually remember that it's been talking all your life, but you have paid it no attention until now.

Get used to watching as many news broadcasts as possible on television, read the newspapers, check out international news on the internet. All this is for you to update yourself on world events because they *will* sneak into your readings and it will be necessary that you recognize them as being unrelated to the intimate experiences of your clients.

Practice: Learning Objectivity—What Do You Really See?

Please set aside a space in an area where you will not be disturbed for the duration of your training time and have a notebook and pen with you for the exercise.

Draw a dot on a clean white sheet of paper in front of where you are sitting.

Sit quietly and look at the dot.

Write down what you *see*.

Realize from the outset that this is not a trick exercise and that, if you are working this exercise with a group, every person's answer will be different.

Your answers will not be:

- Too limited
- An intellectualization
- A personalization
- An esotericisation
- A description of the dot or the paper
- A mental exercise

From my experience with groups, this process can go on for anywhere between one and three hours, and students almost always run the gauntlet of every conceivable emotion from simple frustration to downright rage. This is an excellent way of self-examining one's own motives.

Then, like the *Hundredth Monkey*, one person's overhead light bulb will flash as they realize it's quite possible that the question is not challenging their spiritual understandings or their intelligence, it isn't a trick question, and that there is absolutely no mental activity required. One after the other you will achieve the answers and smiles, as you understand how complicated a simple thing can be made to seem—how much each of you needed to be *right*—and how necessary to the answer your honesty must be.

With Tarot there is no right—there is only telling it as you see it, or hear it or sense it or feel it, even sometimes as you smell it, because all of your senses will come into play—some more than others, depending on your natural talent.

The best way I can think of to describe the answer you will require is to describe a technique employed by martial artists when in a sparring situation with several others: what they do *not* do is to look into the eyes of any opponent, because to do so would trap the person within the identity of the other and they would no longer be able to see the telegraphing of information available through non-focus. Therefore the martial artist will look at nothing and see everything.

UNIT FIVE

From Evolution to Current World Events

Theory: The Tree of Life

The principle of understanding Tarot is based on a foundational understanding of the Tree of Life (also known as Qabbalah), and certain corresponding associations of both astrology and the four elements.

Accuracy at interpreting the prophecies of Tarot, and its wisdom, is dependent on proficiency—there is no guesswork involved with the eventual interpretative function—and the more information you have at hand the easier the work becomes.

With all magical training it is important to initially learn as much as one can. Over time the seeming importance of the accumulated information base peaks and levels out, and you will find that you seem to go the other way; to become simpler, emptier; clear. That'll be because the alchemy factor of the learning has passed the point of its individual parts and becomes who you are rather than what you know.

This work is aimed at assisting you to understand the foundations of magic and the principles of walking between the worlds; to understand that it is both logical and lateral simultaneously…an art and a science. Teaching you to read the cards, however, is the least interesting aspect of this study, albeit the main reason most will have for acquiring this book.

Within the darkness one is waiting—a child of Life, unborn, alone
till the season of confusion when the darkness turns to stone.
The one, the only, covenant that life called from the Crown
will call you when it's ready; when its web is fully spun.

From the forest to the garden
to the desert to the tomb;
to the place of revolution
where no sun has ever shone.

Within the dance of Death's embrace the seed is carried past the Veil;
it is unfolding to its Pattern and a forest is its Grail.
The song, not yet, of what will be; the child of Life is forming
and you'll sing it with each other when it's born within its morning.

From the Forest to the garden
to the desert to the sea,
to the place of resolution . . .
where the child will mother be

and another and another in an endless symphony.
The seed is just one season to the seasons of the Tree
. . . and the Tree is of the Forest of the earth that's yet to be.

—Ly de Angeles, *The Song of Levington Blade*

The Tree of Life is known by other names: Otz Chim; the Asherah Tree; the Ladder of Lights; the Merkabah; Kabbalah[1]; Kabala; the Tree of Knowledge; and Qabbalah (which means "from mouth to ear," indicating an oral tradition of lore).

---

1 Name applied, specifically, to a system of esoteric theosophy which was peculiar to Judaism in Europe after the tenth century. It attained prominence in Spain in the thirteenth century, was disseminated at the time of the expulsion of the Jews from that country, and became identified with Palestine. Its doctrines are contained in the two books "Sefer Yezirah" and "Sefer Zohar."

The Tree is also considered as a star map insofar as it has astrological and planetary associations, the principles and qualities that are important to learn but will only be covered in basic form in this study.

The glyph of the Tree is essentially a system of classification of the various factors that make up both the universe as we know it (macrocosm) and the soul of an individual (microcosm). There are 32 paths on the Tree—10 (numbered) which represent the Sephiroth[2] (spheres/emanations), and 22 Letters (the interlinking paths between the Sephiroth) that also represent the 22 Major Arcana of the Tarot.

Back to the Future (The Theory of Evolution)

In figure 8 you will see the spheres on the glyph of the Tree numbered from base to crown. This is not to be thought of as ascending or descending as is commonly understood, but rather as a noninterrupted process; a systematic expression of one thing, a Songline—and before we get into the associations of a more symbolic nature that will lead you into the Tarot, we approach the Tree of Life in an organic fashion—microcosmically and macrocosmically.

Please note that the journey relevant to both figures 9 and 10 follow what is called the Lightning Flash—a zigzag movement from sphere to sphere—a continuous flow, indivisible and unstoppable.

Microcosmically

Using an actual tree as a model, we can understand the Tree of Life as though from seed to fruit. If you found a seed all alone in the desert, you would have to plant it to know what it is, therefore was, and through observation of the process of its living and dying, what it will be in its cycle. What is powerful is that the pattern of what the seed actually does is encoded within its make-up, and always has been. The seed in this matter is both Malkuth and Kether because they *are*, ultimately, each other—1 being 1^{10} infinitely. We could, therefore, predict that there are only 9 phases to our microcosmic tree because once the tenth phase is realized the fruit has already dropped and another tree is in the process of becoming unique but connected to the pattern of its ancestors.

---

2 Lit. *enumerations*. The Sephiroth are ten emanations of one thing: the Tree.

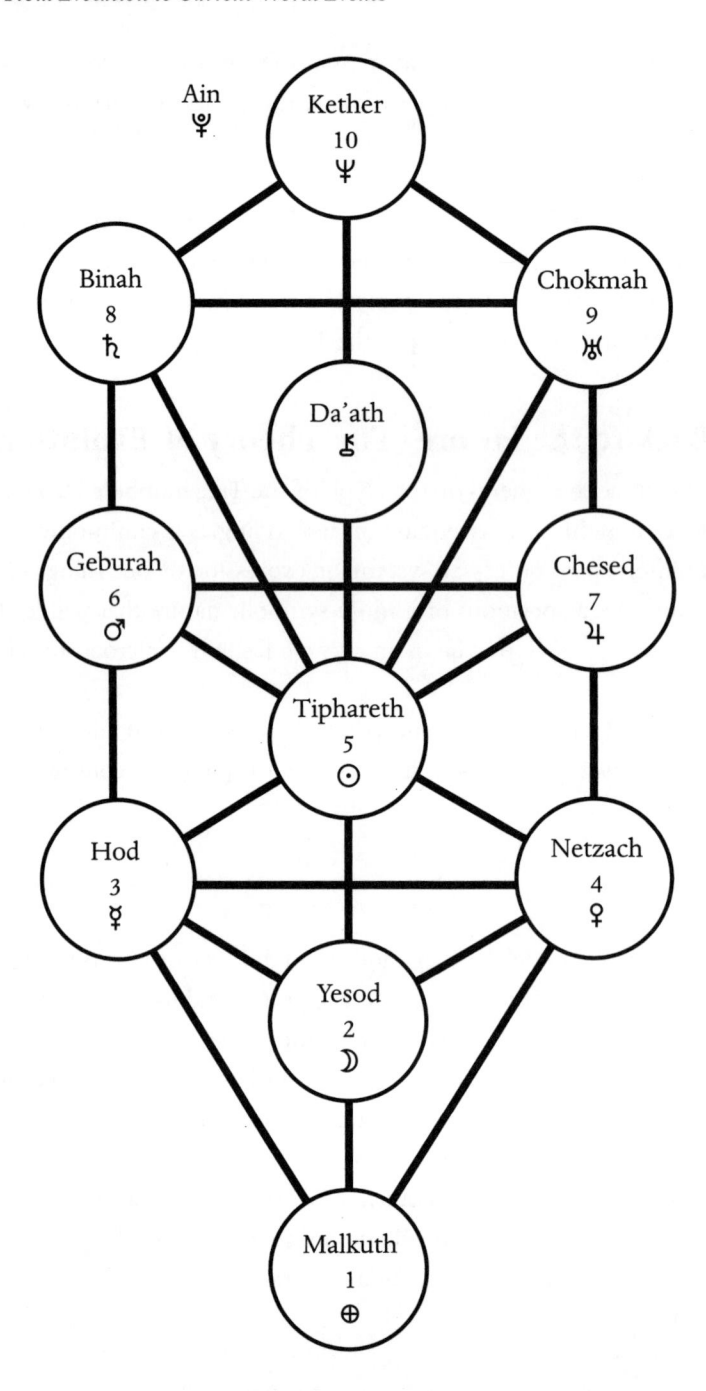

Figure 8: Back to the Future

From seed, to germination, to root, to stem, to leaf, to branch, to bud, to flower, to fruit, to seed, as a plant, is one way of understanding this as is—in the case of the human animal—the principles of the way life seems to progress from conception to death but actually incorporates our entire ancestral lineage unfathomably into both the past and future.

Macrocosmically

(Not including Ice Ages and glaciation periods)

This section is vitally important insofar as not only can we see the probable history of life as we know it unfolding from the vantage of the so-called past, we can—with a fair degree of accuracy—predict how the future will unfold.

Malkuth

When we (Earth) form, we are an inferno of cosmic elemental soup that is so hot that life, as we are to know it in the far-distant future, is not possible. While we slowly cool, solidify, crack, and groan in our upheaval we are seismic to the max, and fry in the poisonous ultra-violet rays of the sun, making things much too hot for even water vapor to possibly form.

Yet we cool.

Then the photosynthesizers among us awake and because of their breathing in, breathing out, excreting, and decaying they add oxygen to our currently toxic atmosphere, causing a layer of ozone to form that successfully blocks out the sun's more lethal effects, setting the stage for life as we understand it, cooling our skin and causing it to crack, forming continents.

Our newly protective atmospheric shield provides water the opportunity to become an active part of us, despite the still violent upheavals and weather patterns, and we become swamp and sea, at the bottom of which—within the warmth of geothermal vents—you and I are seeded.

Hence the symbols of Fire, Air, Earth, and Water—the Four Elements—are the metaphorical rulers of Malkuth.

Yesod

Water, the great warm, wet, lush womb in which we are conceived, forms the greatest content of our individual bodies, and is that upon which all life as we know it depends.

We are now swarming with life that, over time, diversifies and diversifies.

Sometime in the first 700 million years of our existence clouds begin to form in our atmosphere and it starts to rain.

It rains and rains and rains and, affecting the oceans, right along with the procreative cycles of all female mammals, is the pull of our closest orbiting body, the Moon. She waxes and wanes, affecting every tide and every one of us and every living thing.

Some of us move onto the dry land but discover that we cannot journey far from one of our water sources without becoming compost (which, retrospectively, is a good thing).

Hence the Moon is the metaphorical ruler of Yesod.

Hod

Much diversification occurs over millions of years and we are now recognizably people—"homo sapiens sapiens" (although I often wonder about the "wise wise" bit)—and we have realized that fire is useful, as are many other tools. We are nomadic hunter-gatherers and travel the ways of our ancestors, meeting others that through happenstance or circumstance occasionally cross paths with us as we breed in ever-increasing numbers, expanding into wider ranges of territory.

Sometimes we kill them, but sometimes we communicate with them because we have developed language. In certain instances we mate with others and hive off from our clans, diversifying and learning new skills through these cultural interactions. We mimic animal and bird sounds and develop musical instruments and teach others to communicate also.

Hence the metaphorical ruler of Hod is Mercury.

Netzach

What is very certain is that our women are sacred because they give birth—a seemingly miraculous event. We put two and two together and recognize that because Earth nourishes us, it too must be female and we revere her as mother. We are careful never to take more than we need, of course, because there are, within our racial memory, times of flood and famine. Upheavals such as seismic shifts and volcanic eruptions continue to affect us.

We understand that such things as woman, the river, the volcano, the sea, oh, just about everything—especially the territory within which we wander—is sacred, and we must honor them to keep them pleasant and fruitful and beneficent.

There is magic everywhere and our art is what gives it expression, as do certain men and women within the tribe who are gifted at predicting events like the weather and the outcome of the hunt.

This is a time that Rianne Eisler, in *The Chalice and the Blade*, deems "partnership traditions." There is strong evidence to support that throughout the Paleolithic and well into the Neolithic eras, where major advances were made in the fields of agriculture, hunting, the domestication of animals, construction, architecture, art, and technologies, there was, in most European and Near East communities, no imbalance between the sexes.

Hence the metaphorical ruler of Netzach is Venus.

Tiphareth

Someone, sometime, discovers that if good quality seed is harvested from the wild it can be planted and cultivated, providing the family and clan with a ready source of food as long as the family and clan stays around long enough to protect the resource. Then someone else works out that we can do the same thing with certain animals.

As these techniques gain in popularity and people feel more secure because they are better fed—even down to having surplus in abundant years—an entirely unprecedented culture emerges.

Hierarchies come into existence based on wealth: the greatest surplus or the biggest herd of domesticated cattle providing for others in times of scarcity and, along with them, for the first time in historical record, came the new mystics—full-time, professional temple priests complete with processes of initiation into inner mysteries and sciences. These are the sorcerers and prophets of the Netzachian period who are now acknowledged in the archives of history because records are kept—in art, architecture, writing, trade, and household goods.

Controlled religion and ritual become the norm, along with a warrior class trained to protect the interests of the region.

Ritual by the season and the stars is practiced, with the god/king wedded to the land (a goddess/queen) whereby he is metaphorically (sometimes not) sacrificed yearly through the scything of the grain, and we enter the time of sacerdotal ritual death.

All this can historically be placed somewhere between the Paleolithic era, which goes back over 30,000 years, and the Neolithic, over 10,000 years ago.

During this period, and that which follows, orders of gods and goddesses attain human-like status, and temples and sacred architecture become the centers of these civilizations.

The era of sacrificed kings dawns, where the gods of grain are sacrificed annually and explicit solar and stellar calendars (controlled and understood by the priesthood and the wise) guide the people in the techniques of farming, while the sun and the stars and the whole of the natural world become a plethora of gods and goddesses. The master-anything appears on the main stage, from blacksmith to scribe, and individual achievement is capable of raising an individual to that stature . . . or that of a god.

Hence the metaphorical ruler of Tiphareth is the Sun, the one and only centre of the known universe.

Geburah

Bearing in mind that we are still experiencing the aftereffects of the last Ice Age—particularly in the far north of Earth—it is now the period of the destruction of the current way of life, a thing from which we have yet to recover.

It is the time of invasion.

Geburah's metaphorical ruler is Mars, and this planet has more than one quality about it. It is known to the majority as the planet that represents strife and war, but that is only one aspect of it. The other is the family, clan, and/or territory, and our capacity to guard and defend against harm.

During this phase of the human animal amongst us were wave after wave of incursions and cultural upheavals and the introduction of male gods of war and mountains—gradually imposing their ideologies and ways of living and thinking on the lands and people they conquered.

One thing that unites these invading hegemonies is the model of *Might is Right*—the morality of domination—and the other is the suppression of women.

I will speculate that the trend came about with the recession of the previous Ice Age. Imagine if you will a climate wherein mere survival is a day-to-day struggle, where the elements themselves are your enemies and where the mortality rate in often sub-zero temperatures affects the very young and the very old. Imagine that the hunter must fight anyone and anything invading his territory and that surviving offspring will ensure food on the table in later years, particularly if they are strong males. Imagine, then, the need to keep both one's mate and one's children very closely controlled to ensure none of your enemies steal them to increase their own stock. Lynn Margulis and Dorion Sagan explore this theme deeply in their 1991 work *Mystery Dance, On the Evolution of Human Sexuality*.

The *unnaturalness* (author's emphasis) of the need to control, dominate, and subdue women by force seems to be the product of an ancient desperation carried into the future unnecessarily by these warlike invaders, into the conquered regions and assimilated through habit.

So Geburah becomes recognized as the advent of a warlike, dominating, *Might is Right* period of recognizable history that is refined over time, eradicating individuality among its warriors, entrenching the species with entire hierarchies and empires utterly determined to take what others have, debase them as weak or inferior (for losing the war!), and rape their resources.

Sound familiar? Of course! We are entering into very familiar territory.

Chesed

Here we are in a history so recently unfolding that we can say without doubt that it will continue to be the dominant paradigm well into the future.

The ruler—Jupiter—is a planet of expansion (among other things).

With the advent of dominant empires come their religious hierarchies—monotheist religious hierarchies because, to quote the movie *Highlander*, "There can be only one!"—proselytizing exclusivity, beginnings and endings, revelation or damnation.

But side by side walks scientific curiosity, philosophical debate, artistic excellence, medical advances, and exploration beyond narrow or regional confines. Seafaring cultures such as the Norse, the Phoenicians, the Chinese, and the indigenous people of the Americas link the world.

Communities move from localized councils of elders to governing regimes equipped with military supremacy, overriding others' cultures (not necessarily a good thing, we have discovered), always hand-in-glove with religious autonomy.

We are taught that this is progress, that expansion of empires opens up trade between many nations. It's a lie, really, because that has gone on for thousands of years—uncountable thousands of years—only now the records are kept in a controlled fashion, written by the hand of the scribes of the conquerors.

This is still the case, but we're moving, in our current era, across what on the Tree of Life is called the Abyss—the only place on the glyph where there is no recognized path along the Lightning Flash. We are transiting what is called Da'ath heading for Binah—a world that will be utterly different from what has been known in any historical context thus far.

The very fact that Binah is a continuation of the process already described as making up the Macrocosmic Tree informs us that *it is already known* because it has happened before; that it is destiny.

Binah

So how long will the transition take? These transitions are the same as for anything—there is no date where growth is concerned because it is in a continuous process of maturation. Basically we can see the effects of Binah flowing to us out of every headline and every news bulletin, because Binah is metaphorically ruled by Saturn.

This has traditionally been called the planet of limitations but, and more to the point, Saturn *defines* limitations (which are somewhat illusory in reality). It is the planet of boundaries, time, and structure, and when our structure is threatened, fear is often created.

What do we see happening worldwide at the moment?

On a planetary level, we are seeing the presumed predictability of weather patterns and Earth itself—which in the past we, as a species, have relied upon to remain consistent—falter and change in drastic and dramatic ways, so much so that when we read about tsunamis, earthquakes, and hurricanes, polar ice melts, and prolonged, vicious drought, we do so with increased alarm, as in our current history these things have not been known to be as numerous or intense.

New laws (often draconian) are being written and implemented to clamp down on threats, real or potential, with increased powers given to both law enforcement and the military, with spyware devices the norm, and censorship of freedom-of-information severely imposed.

Resources that have always been the inalienable, sustainable right of all species are becoming privatized in ever more costly and controlling ways (a hundred years ago who would have thought water could be commodified), corporations become the new theocracies, with money and the market as their gods.

Fundamentalist religions dominate earlier-won liberalizations, threatening us with a return to Inquisition-Age morality.

We enter into a time of institutionalized everything, of centralized information data banks that, most likely, will require tattooed or implanted bar-coding of our very identities, increased imprisonment for *possible* crimes, increased security with Big Brother watching from a camera on every street corner, rationing of once previously easily available commodities like gasoline and its many byproducts to controlled breeding (not necessarily a bad thing) and designer babies. Sanctions, refugees both urban and continent-wide, debt, the threat of epidemic, increased monopolization of financial powers, and decreases in power for the masses are now commonplace.

To offset these events we will see social upheaval on an unprecedented scale as the above effects bite into the pocket of the average person, threatening in a way not seen since the Great Depression, as work becomes scarce and more selective with the increases in the *technologicization* of culture and an expanding underworld of secret cabals and black-market-everything removes even the possibility of the surety of stability.

Sound familiar? Of course it does—it doesn't take a psychic to inform you what you already know—but unfortunately the time- span has just begun.

Binah is traditionally known by the description: UNDERSTANDING. This time, other than being restraining, restricting, categorizing, and institutionalizing, Binah also engenders the opposite: rebellion, liberation, the journey to the depths of anything seeking understanding by those who live in secluded autonomy outside of the walls of acceptability—who choose to live as outlaws. We are likely to see an entire network of contra-band information-trafficking as world events are edited for consumption and an uprising of Earth-sustaining alternative enclaves seek release from enforced paradigms.

And sooner or later the realization—the understanding—of the ramifications of our actions will take us into a new phase, whether we like it or not. Whether that is another Ice Age or something entirely different will depend on *natural* cycles rather than humanity's megalomaniacal idea of its own superiority.

Keep faith, however, because of what follows.

I have not mentioned any of the twenty-two paths that link the Sephiroth, but I shall do so now because what follows is prophetically most enlightening. The path that links Binah to Chokmah on this journey is The Empress card, astrologically ruled by Venus with the Hebrew letter ד Daleth (meaning Door) representing it.

Not only that, but Chokmah is ruled by Uranus, the planet most associated with technology, so there will assuredly be a strong link between what happens during the time of Binah and what happens during the reign of Chokmah.

Chokmah

We are now in uncharted territory because the events from hereon, and until Malkuth initiates another revolution (after another fashion), are not within our racial or documented archives . . . but there are clues.

Cargo Cult Theory: The Cargo Cult is one of a number of religious movements, chiefly in Melanesia, that first appeared in the late nineteenth century, but were particularly prevalent during and after World War II, with the apparently miraculous dropping of supplies from airplanes. Adherents believe in the imminent arrival of material goods, or cargo, by supernatural agents such as tribal gods or ancestral spirits. In anticipation, temples rendered like airplanes are constructed, landing strips, wharves, warehouses, and other elaborate preparations for receiving the cargo are often made, and normal activities such as gardening cease, stocks of food are destroyed, and current customs are abandoned. These preparations prophesy the end of the old order and the arrival of a new age of freedom and plenty.

These attitudes are not restricted to so-called primitive tribal people living in the highlands of New Guinea—they are the theologies of most Messianic and Rapturist[3] cults.

It's a bit of a *Von Danikinist* theory (one that does *not* involve any reference to extraterrestrial activity) that takes into account the many arcane doctrines of fiery machines, haloed messengers, seeming atomic explosions, and acacia-wood boxes containing mysteriously engraved stones that could kill as though by electrocution.

It is possible that technology was once as advanced, in its own way (before the onset of the last Ice Age) as it is today . . . and that not everyone on the planet was necessarily affected by that frosty event. In the Northern Hemisphere there are hundreds of documented accounts of people/beings that once upon a time lived underground, in the underworld—from Europe with its legends of anything from Dwarves to the Sídhe, to the Central Anatolian Plateau with its bizarre Cappadocian "Fairy Chimneys," from Africa and the towering cliff cities (Bandiagara) of the Dogon and Petra in Jordan, to the carved cliff-cities of the Pueblos.

---

3 Rapture:
    a. The state of being transported by a lofty emotion; ecstasy.
    b. An expression of ecstatic feeling. Often used in the plural.
    c. *The transporting of a person from one place to another, especially to heaven* (italics are mine).

There are countless myths and legends (that are not inventions but *must* stem from a remembered, if distorted, historic reference) of people or messengers that flew, that arrived in fiery chariots, that brought the gifts of fire, the spoken word, and countless technologies.

The knowledge of astronomy and the tendency of ancient races to build towering edifices, both to mirror constellations and to allow them to be nearer to their gods, is not so far fetched when we consider what kind of effect dynamic cataclysm would have on entire generations who found themselves in virtually primitive conditions, the only way of preserving history being through oral retelling that could conceivably end up being like Chinese Whispers[4].

Chokmah is also given the title *Sphere of the Zodiac* and is called the Sephiroth of Wisdom.

Wisdom is a quality of fulfillment that is the outcome of three distinct steps: experience, knowledge, and understanding. It cannot be gained otherwise. It is as though—if we take the history of every stage of the Tree up to this point—Earth herself has benefited from all that has gone before and is at the stage of fulfillment necessary to transform herself into her next phase of life.

Or to become another Earth.

Consider the possibilities:

- Either we develop the technology to enable us to create a kind of "ark" capable of carrying the genetic keys (of life as we know it) out into the universe, encoded to seek whatever environmental field is ultimately able to sustain it, or
- We have another Ice Age, due to global warming or other natural catastrophe and the experience, knowledge, understanding, and wisdom go underground, only to surface in either actuality or memory in an appropriate future.

In describing the qualities of Uranus, Bernard Casimir says, *"It can be like the Lightning-struck Tower in the Tarot insofar as its eruptive and 'destructive' blatancy can be as dangerous as exposed electrical wiring to wet hands in a thunderstorm! It is, however, the power of the urge for differentiation and the revolution of independent consciousness."*

---

4 The phenomenon known as Chinese Whispers stems from the game of the same name. When passing information from one party to another (usually verbally) the facts and theme often become distorted.

Kether

Governed by the planet Neptune is the dream, the inspiration, the unknowable, the true term "Occult." Neptune has been termed the "Universal Solvent" and whatever Uranus has destroyed or blasted, Neptune dissolves. It is both the sleep of the seed in the womb of the fruit that rots as it nourishes and the ocean of either space or the newly birthing Earth wherein all memory of its parents are as embedded as the knowledge of forever is embedded in our own DNA. Called *The Crown,* it is where all that precedes it comes together in an instant of exquisite, orgasmic enlightenment or awareness, like all the light bulbs coming on at once and where the world says, *"Oh, so this is what life is all about!"*

The Tarot is this great wheel of seeming repetition that is, in itself, an illusion because nothing truly ever repeats itself but merely appears to . . . while the truism that the only absolute is change applies here perfectly.

A Word about Da'ath: Da'ath is an enigma. Everything I have ever read tells me that it is both there and not there; it both is and is not a Sephirah. Yet it is said to represent knowledge. I have relegated Chiron to this sphere because it is not a planet, yet it is most definitely a force to be reckoned with astrologically.

Da'ath is nestled within the abyss of the Tree and is affected by two paths: that of the Empress and that of the High Priestess. This, in itself, is profound.

Da'ath represents knowledge not found in any traditional way. Like a flash of inspiration it assures you that you already know the message that it brings, but from elsewhere.

In a Tarot spread the card that sits here is called a key—it is something already known but not recognized as such.

Barbara Hand Clow has dubbed Chiron *The Rainbow Bridge,* indicating that it is that which links body and soul, but body and soul are—like the centaur—already one thing. Da'ath, as you will read further on, is the bridge between what is called the *Ruach* and the *Neschamah.* It is as though messages from the Deep—from the gods and their avatars—pass through this portal, instructing or guiding us toward the Supernals of understanding, wisdom, and enlightenment (Kether).

We need only recognize its genius hidden within experience, like the butterfly effect in *Chaos Theory,* whereby everything we thought of as real changes through painful and undesirable events—often the only thing capable of shattering complacency.

The effect of the convergence of the Empress and High Priestess cards previously mentioned gives us a strong indication, not only of humanity's ongoing attitude toward both women and the goddesses, but of Earth herself. As the Empress card she is bountiful, providing all species with all other species as food and shelter, but when she is raging with hurricanes and earthquakes and the occasional tsunami, she is vilified as "The Bitch"—nature requiring conquering. The High Priestess card is akin to that ship of the desert as she moves from Tiphareth across the vast empty landscape of Mystery and ancient buried forests on her voyage to Kether, carrying necessities and trusting in her own endurance to get her to her destination (where she already is).

This tells me that knowledge is immeasurable and exists in the very air we breathe and in places unseen. Like a passage across a trackless wasteland traveled since forever, it never goes away; and like seeds buried within the desert sands, the vast glacial permafrost, or miles deep beneath arctic ice, they await only their season.

Practice: The Making of a Template and First Use of Major Arcana

The exercise for this unit is to purchase a piece of poster-size white cardboard and to draw up your own glyph of the Tree, incorporating all the associations you have available in this unit. You could, if you choose, embellish the drawing with the traditional planetary colors, which are:

Malkuth (the four traditional Elementals)—olive, russet, citrine, black

Yesod (Moon)—purple or violet

Hod (Mercury)—orange

Netzach (Venus)—emerald green

Tiphareth (Sun)—yellow or gold

Geburah (Mars)—red or crimson

Chesed (Jupiter)—sapphire blue

Binah (Saturn)—indigo

Chokmah (Uranus)—grey or silver

Kether (Neptune)—white

Da'ath (Chiron)—brilliant light blue

And you could also add the Tarot card associations that are shown in the following illustration (figure 9).

Having done this, it is time to take out your pack of Tarot cards and separate the Minors from the Majors, putting the Minor Arcana to one side and shuffling the Majors.

Simply lay out one card after the other, in order of the Lightning Flash, from Malkuth to Kether, and write up the layout in your journal.

What you are doing at this stage is contemplating the correlation between your understanding of the Tree of Life and the theoretical concept of evolution that you have just studied, knowledge of how the planetary ideas fit in with this, and your own gut feelings and intuition regarding what card falls where.

This is a short-term, non-personal, macrocosmic spread. You can refer to the possible interpretation of each card that is written up later (see Unit 8) or you can simply get a feeling.

If, for example, you were to lay the Tower card in the sphere of Hod, the ramifications of a news broadcast pertinent to a train accident or car bombing would be obvious. If the same card fell in Netzach you would hear of anything from an environmental disaster to the death sentence of a woman for supposed crimes against morality under Islam's extremist Shari'a Law.

Please only do this exercise occasionally. The earlier suggestion to watch evening news broadcasts will tell you the outcome of the predictions.

Using this artistic template for Tree of Life spreads will assist you to learn the associations quickly.

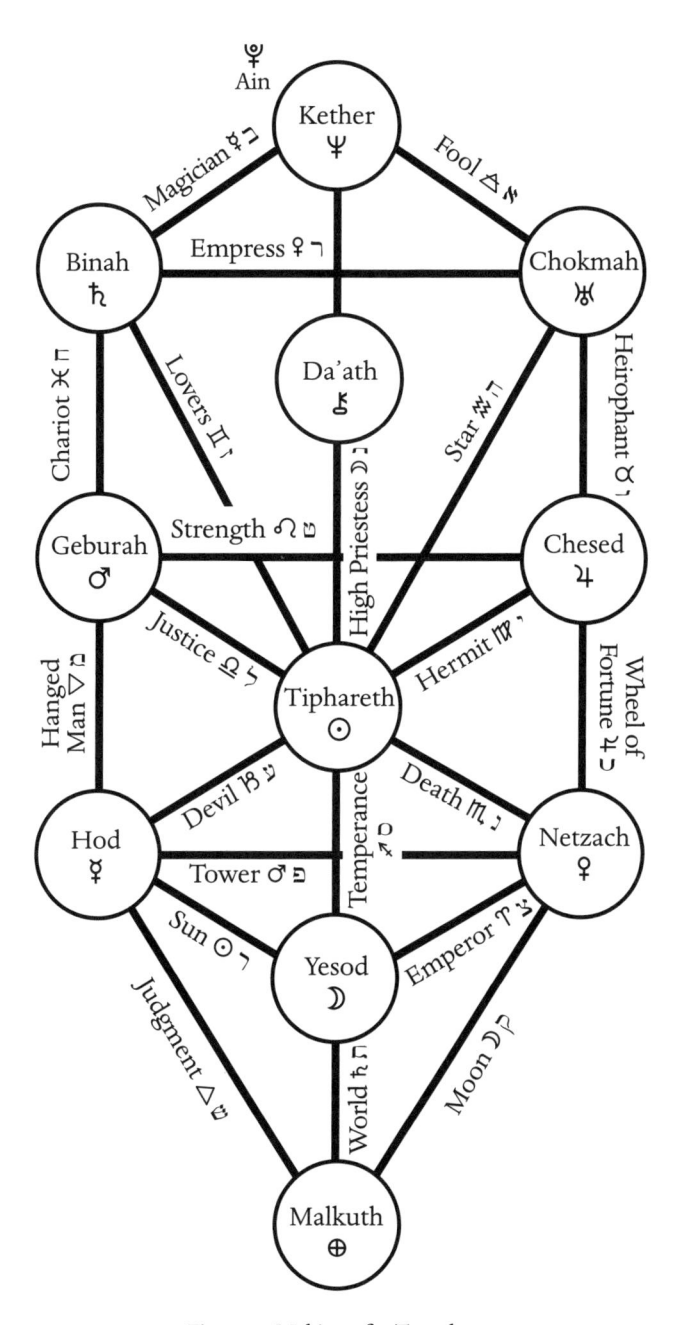

Figure 9: Making of a Template

UNIT SIX

The Infinite and the Individual

Theory: From No-thing to Something—
The Individual and the Tree of Life

In figure 8 the numbering of the Sephiroth was from Malkuth (1) to Kether (10). In most texts you will find the standard formula to be the other way around because of the perennial concepts of heaven and earth, and the religiosity of the Tree. These are not our concerns here, but the next image of the Tree of Life (figure 10) is depicted this way so you can become comfortable with any sequence at all.

This is important because it is necessary to consider the Tree as endless, because it does not simply represent one thing or one event (even though, paradoxically, it also does) and because it cannot be limited in any way. It is as much your personal family tree as it is the movement of global cultures, the rise and fall of empires and the movement of any event, from conception to apparent conclusion, from education and relationships to birth, death, and all in between.

In its more mystical sense we can evoke the numerical sequence and multiply it infinitely because, in truth, what we perceive (in the stylized glyph) is only Malkuth (or any of the others). Within each Sephirah there exists another Tree within which other Trees can be calculated infinitely, and the outward journey is the journey from a spark (Kether), or conception, of both you and of everything that eventuates in the inevitable expression of material reality (Malkuth).

This is a way to contemplate both time and personal experience.

The Individual

This figure (figure 10) is the microcosmic you, the individual, in relation to everything.

Nephesh

On the Tree this is represented by Malkuth.

This is the material, physical you; your body. Your body is remarkable as it allows tactile and sensory experience. It is your foundation—your mortal representation within life as you know it … and you are an outcome of the passage of time, having present within yourself the DNA of each and every one of your ancestors as well as the evolutionary experience that goes way beyond our understanding of what makes us human, such as: the same iron (within the hemoglobin) that was present at the moment of the theoretical big bang, the same hydrogen, the same oxygen.

Many people are unconscious of the workings of the body, which is often detrimental to its maintenance. The body, however, is remarkable in that it operates even without conscious recognition of its greatest works: healing wounds through the creation of new cells; split-second reactions; memory; and the extraordinary workings of the nervous system.

You were always going to be who you are, and the journey of this life of yours has been happening since Kether (on the outward-moving Tree), which is both your physical conception and the conception of the universe.

But are you your body? Of *course* you are—it's just that you are so much more than that or you wouldn't make sense. You are your experiences.

You are also intimately connected to any environment in which you find yourself so that, to all intents and purposes, you are also your environment and each of us responds in mutuality to the places we live and visit.

When in relation to the Tarot, Malkuth represents—bodily—the person's feet and legs. Injury or health in relation to these body parts will show up when you look at the Tree of Life spread as will the environment in which clients will find themselves. This is not

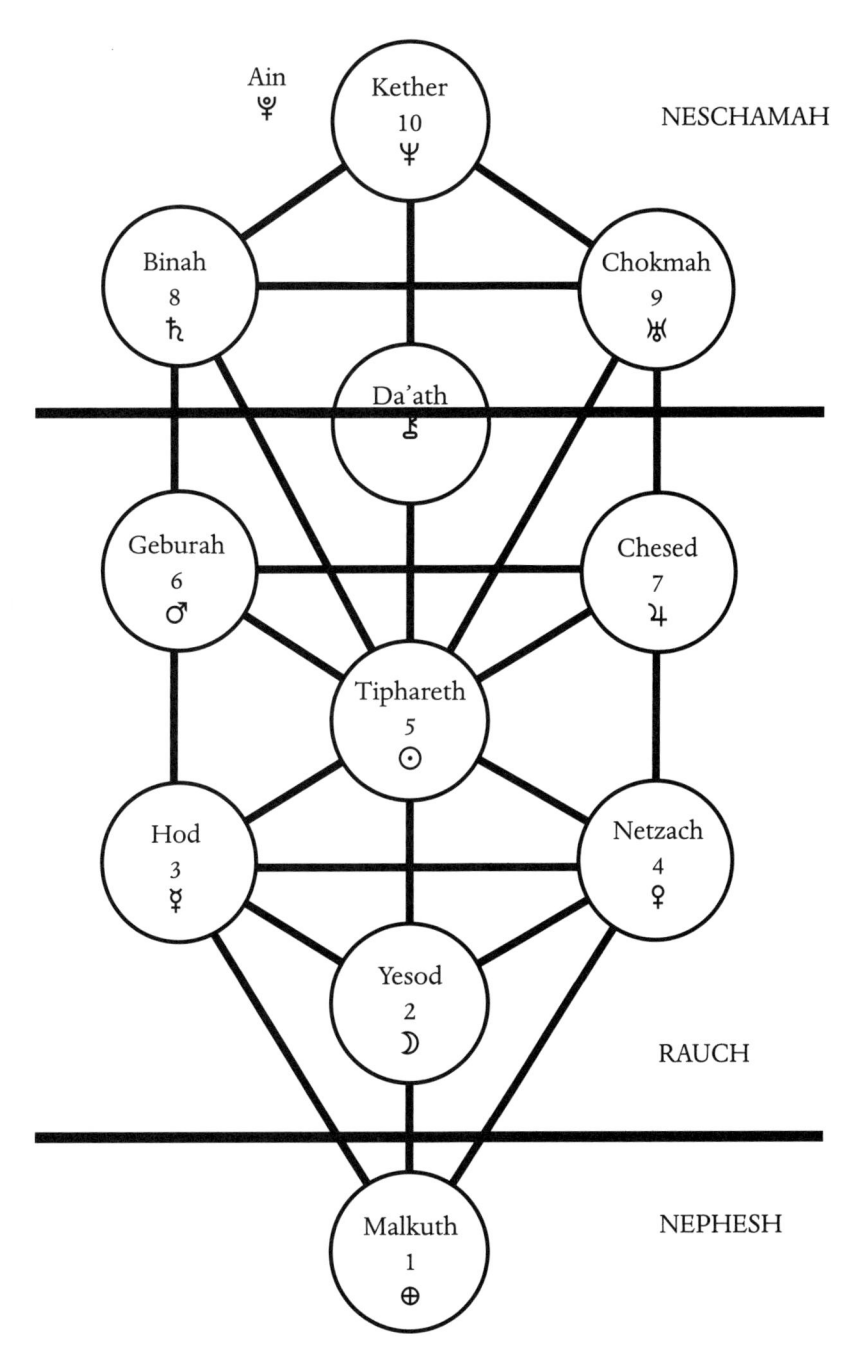

Figure 10: The Individual

merely the actual place or abode but can often also represent the sensory experience: the spread may show, for example, the 7 of Cups and this will tell you that the client does not know where they belong; it may show the Ace of Cups, which tells you that their environment is a place of love or that they love where they will be. The Empress card, however, expresses both a lush, tropical environment and/or a place of beauty (as is understood by the client).

Ruach

Tiphareth

Self-Awareness—the centre of the Ruach is Tiphareth, like a sun around which revolve many planets. That's you. It's you in the world. You are the product of your experiences and they are continuous (even though you are so much more than that).

In the Tree of Life spread, the card that falls here represents who the client is, but if viewing the spread for health purposes, health or vulnerability relates to the vital organs of heart, liver, pancreas, spleen, kidneys, lungs.

Yesod

This is the Sephirah of instinct. It is stimuli at an animal level, from sexual arousal to fear to laughter to despair, and it is also your racial and inherited traits. It is your connection to everything else and therefore it is your psychic and intuitive nature. Your primal urges and your stored memories are the Yesodic experience and therefore it's also been deemed both the subconscious and the unconscious (but what are these really?) It is the treasure house of archetypes and the secret of your own mind. Yesod is experiential but not necessarily from external stimuli.

In a Tree of Life spread, when looking at physical health issues, Yesod represents the genitals, the reproductive system, the lower back and the sciatic nerve, as well as the health of the mind.

Hod

Hod represents intercommunication with things and people; the way you express yourself, your capacity to learn, the languages of the world—everything from human language to that of traffic and thunder and what they teach you; where you travel and how, what comes your way, the physically changing world; from your daily journey to check the mailbox; from any moving vehicle or dwelling, to the internet and interstate or world travel.

It is everything ever said to you or that you hear. Everything you will ever read or write, and the ability to learn, is the result of the experience of Hod.

In the Tree of Life spread, when looking at all things physical, Hod represents the left hip.

Netzach

Your experience of all that is beautiful, sensual, tactile, artistic, or fecund are Netzachian experiences. Your ability to think laterally is governed by this Sephirah as is your sense of appreciation of all that is unbridled and erotic in nature.

Every time you enjoy sex, dance, give birth to anything from human children to poetry, you are affected by Netzach. Whenever you add your own artistic touch to the world, you are both enhancing your own experiences and feeding the experiences of others. The same applies when you work in the dirt, planting or playing, for the "green thumb" is an attribute of Venus' influence.

In the Tree of Life spread—physically—Netzach represents the right hip.

Chesed

As much as the ability to learn is the experience of Hod, so the information and the knowledge collected, explored, transmitted throughout the world is the experience of Chesed. So also is the spiritual or religious experience, the deeper understanding implied by philosophical thought, and your own inspiration to add to what is already in the world.

Chesed is the experience of you in the world—not so much the individual as the deeds, for much of your life they are how the world will know you.

Education of any kind dwells at the heart of Chesed, not merely the book-learned kind, but the kind that changes you, demands that you grow, and requires you to interact with others in your community, either locally or macrocosmically for the experience of interaction and sociability.

Chesed is your work, or your vocation, projected outward and experienced in the world and all that comes from it.

On a physical level—when viewing the Tree of Life spread—Chesed represents the left shoulder, arm, and hand.

Geburah

This is the experience of excitation, more physical than intellectual, and related to many things from martial arts to the preservation of the rights and liberties of clan, tribe, community, and culture.

It is your ability to defend what you know to be right.

In the current era this task has fallen almost solely onto the police or armed forces and we find ourselves more and more in dire physical straits accompanied by the social and health dysfunctions that accompany the "toothless.[1]"

Geburah, affected as it is by Mars, is too often relegated to the idea of aggression or warlike attributes, but is this necessarily the case? It is very uncommon for one species to invade the territory of another, and, even though a wasp will invade a bee hive, it does so at great peril, for the bees will swarm and die rather than allow senseless slaughter or abuse of their home.

Any animal or species will do the same. It is natural. Therefore your physical fitness is linked—other than to a life well lived—to your experience of personal power in the world.

Your competitive nature is experienced here, as are all adrenalin-triggered responses.

On a physical level—when viewing the Tree of Life spread—Geburah represents the right shoulder, arm, and hand.

All five Sephiroth (Yesod, Hod, Netzach, Geburah and Chesed) are experienced all the time, even in deep states of meditation or contemplation. While there is self-awareness—while there is life (and as has already been said "When is there no life?")—you, as the experience of Tiphareth at the heart of the Ruach, are perennial, because knowledge is only *understood* when there is an experiential framework, even if imagined theoretically.

Neschamah

The whole is greater than the sum of its parts . . . but the sum of its parts is also the whole.[2]

The Neschamah consists of Binah, Chokmah, and Kether, called the *Supernals*, and they are (personally) Mind. They are the depths of you, the wisdom-voices within you that are

---

1 Those who have lost the ability to defend themselves or to be self-sufficient.
2 This quote is attributed to Aristotle.

sometimes yours and sometimes those of the gods that utilize your perceptions and your inner mansions as their gateway.

We begin with the mystical Da'ath, which is neither the Ruach nor Neschamah but is *Something Else Elsewhere,* and there is no access to the Neschamah unless at some time in your life the experience of Da'ath has been triggered.

This triggering could as easily be a profound dream, a saying, a singular conversation, the impact of which—if you allow it—alters your entire life-perspective, resulting in the birth of the Questioner within you that will challenge every paradigm and truism and that will have you communicating with these gods, no matter who or what you perceive them to be. What I know is that once this trigger is activated *they* will come to *you* through recognition.

The possibility is there for all people, yet many dare not take the chance because of the threat of being considered different that overshadows many cultures, and that possibility—that umbilicus—is the High Priestess card that perpetually links you to the Source as it journeys from Tiphareth to Kether.

Binah (also known as Neschamah Proper) is the gate of Time and Matter. She is like the treasure house of all that exists; the Hall of Records of Life infinitely in all directions and none, while Chokmah is the energy that is the principle upon which all life is founded, the absolute of vitality.

Kether, however, is the deepest, most mysterious centre of the circle (see figure 11), the inner star, the pebble in the pool that drops infinitely through everything, causing concentric ripples everywhere simultaneously.

One shouldn't consider the centre of anything to be the smallest ratio of the greater manifestation because there would *be* no greater manifestation without that infinite point—therefore it is huge beyond imagining because it holds within itself the pattern of everything, including what it was and what it will be.

The key to contact with this natural realm is listening for other, and more, than our own voices.

On a biological level Da'ath represents the throat, larynx, thyroid, mouth and neck; Binah represents the right shoulder and ear; Chokmah, the left shoulder and ear plus the nervous system; whereas Kether represents the head in general, the brain in particular.

Practice: Using the Template and All Cards to Decode Individual and Public Events

Using the template you have made, please take the whole pack and shuffle the cards. This time, however, you will lay them out, in order of the Lightning Flash, from Kether to Malkuth.

This is where it gets interesting because when you have laid them out you will not know exactly *who* the sequence represents! They can be telling you information about anyone from your best friend to the president of a country . . . even the fate of a country itself.

Again record the cards and their positions in your journal because what is certain is that sooner or later who or what the spread represents will become apparent.

You can go to the section of this book that gives certain meanings to the cards and consider them in relationship with their placement on the template, but remember to keep your objectivity, realizing that the prediction is not going to be for you.

If you are working with a group while training take turns, but each person must use their own cards.

This kind of a scenario is where Tarot gets cheeky! Throughout all the *Walking the Web* workshops this practice has always alluded to someone in the group and I see no reason to doubt it will do the same for your own. Only time will tell for whom.

Look at the Tree of Life spread from three perspectives:

1. experiential
2. emotional
3. physical

UNIT SEVEN

The Soul's Journey

Theory: The Major Arcana and the Cycles of the Personal Tree of Life

Tarot is a living myth and as such it mirrors the patterns of change that occur in all organic life forms, most obviously our own. As such, it is a key to guiding the individual, family, or nation through what can sometimes be confusing and seemingly treacherous times. The Major Arcana both represent and evoke this. If we take each of their traditional images into account we can see and understand this much better and we need to see these in a numerically sequenced circle spread (figure 11) for it to be recognized.

72 Unit Seven: The Soul's Journey

Figure 11: The Soul's Journey

The First Phase—"I am the Parent Tree": CHALLENGE

    0 Fool

    1 Magician

    2 High Priestess

    3 Empress

    4 Emperor

    5 Hierophant

    6 Lovers

    7 Chariot

    8 Strength

9 Hermit

10 Wheel of Fortune

11 Justice

The Second Phase—"Dropping from the Parent Tree": INDIVIDUATION

12 Hanged Man

13 Death

14 Temperance

15 Devil

16 Tower

17 Star

18 Moon

19 Sun

20 Judgement

21 World

The First Phase—"I am the Parent Tree": CHALLENGE

A cycle of time (any cycle of time) follows the pattern of the circle of cards in a clockwise fashion thus:

The Fool is a mere moment; a seemingly irrelevant, seemingly inconsequential, seemingly random, barely registered moment. It always takes that, you know, for a cycle of events to activate and it's *meant* to go unnoticed because very often we reject change out of fear that, whatever it may bring, life will not be the same in retrospect. So we don't notice what could only be called a quickening. That's the start. If we look at it like a human life, it is the moment of conception, the parent that conceives and, the Fool card being what it is—a blind card—the inability to glean the consequences. Whether the fetus progresses to birth and life, or is miscarried or aborted, is irrelevant at this stage because, still, the cycle will fulfill itself, both for the parent and the unborn. All of it is destiny in one way or another.

The Magician is when the awakened cycle is recognized and/or realized. For the parent it is the moment of the understanding of the state of pregnancy and, again, whether the pregnancy reaches full term or not, the person's life will never be the same. Should the pregnancy reach full term and an infant be the result, the Magician card represents the power of this seeming new beginning.

Released from the comfort of the amniotic sea, the offspring emerges into an utterly unknown environment, alien and sensory.

They have an ability—these new lives (which are not always biological)—to affect and control people and events around them by their very presence. No matter how transitory, or seemingly simple, a new experience is always awesome; a moment to be seized and remembered by any who participate.

Whether it is the birth of the child, moving to an altogether new location, achieving an educational degree, leaving a relationship and stepping out alone into the world, or the first page of a book you are to write, it's all the same. No matter how much fear, no matter what the attending emotion, there are endless possibilities, limitless variations to how we can experience this new thing.

Upon the altar of the Magician card are the ritual symbols of the four elements of Earth, Air, Fire, and Water, indicating that all that one needs is available; all that is required for their use is intention. The Magician points above and below and, despite the common term of "As above, so below, after another fashion," I now realize that what this figure is also saying is that Kether and Malkuth are different aspects of each other, perpetually linked and one thing—the Magician, in his or her own right, represents the songline of forever.

The High Priestess is the mystery of the unknown that faces the newborn. In some way it is obvious that the knowledge to progress is inherent within that mystery. It is the "not-knowing" time; the wondering time. Whether it is the child's inability to name and understand objects, people, everything, or whether it is the time of learning when the answers to our questions remain in the excited state of being unanswered (occulted) or the first flutterings of the possible intimacy of the newly-met hints at sensuality or love, all is interwoven with the High Priestess card where there are environment; a world of mystery that is *not* the product of logic and rationalism, and cannot be understood in this manner. In the Llewellyn Tarot deck there is a secret even within the image: if you look closely you will see that the so-called Inner Sanctum, which many claim that the priestess guards the entry to, is actually an outside environment—the curtain obscuring an exit to a world beyond; the ocean glimpsed behind her, not some deep chamber. The observer/participant is *already* on the inside; has not yet left some cloistered environment; has not yet awoken to the fullness of life, the cycle, the experience.

The Empress. Mother! For the infant it is the moment of the nipple, the moment of first nurture when abandonment, rejection, and death are allayed. The Empress card represents the good things, the luscious things: the first meal in a foreign country, the flush of requited intimacy, the moment we take to bathe in an achievement that is realized. The Empress is a form of reciprocation—always the pleasure of a thing shared is beautiful, and the Empress is Beauty—not in any stylized fashion or form but in an utter lack of pretense: art, love, tactile pleasure, fecundity, sensual erotic environments, nourishment.

For the newborn, the Empress is whoever or whatever fulfills its needs. At this stage of its life it has no modesty, no consciousness of morality or embarrassment and it will eat, bawl, defecate, vomit, or burp to its heart's content—things, sadly, that it will unlearn very soon.

The Emperor is the crossover between learning and unlearning. It is where structure is imposed on the child. It is when the mystery begins to concretize into tables and chairs, rooms, recognized faces, remembered experience through repetition. This is the time the child learns to crawl, walk, talk, potty-train, sleep in its own bed, is spoken to endlessly in the adult's need to have it understand the consensual world. Order is imposed. Education is the method. This is the beginning, within this cycle, of that which will continue endlessly and ceaselessly: learning.

The Emperor is, as I have already mentioned, order. Therefore it is all that falls within this category from informal and formal education to government bodies, established traditions, propriety within the consensual morality of family, community, nation; acceptable behavior, manners, status. It represents the rules and regulations imposed upon individuality and all aspects of the previously (and currently) experienced Arcanum. Whereas the Empress represents "mother" (in whatever fashion), so the Emperor represents "father" in traditional fashion rather than currently transitional role representation, which—from my perspective—is rather sad. This representation, while remaining entrenched in many cultures and societies worldwide even in this, the twenty-first century, remains an onerous archetype that many men would reject if they could, while others cling to it frantically, to the detriment of true humanitarianism and compassion.

That leads us to *The Hierophant*. At this stage I'd like to conjecture that again, in chicken-and-egg fashion, when society changes beyond the recognizable paradigms that have been erected and maintained for the last ten thousand years, so will the images that Tarot requires to represent itself also change. There is a vast variety of Tarot-like decks of cards on the market today, despite the continually overriding evidence that the traditional images hold true to the ways of humanly structured behavior, and it seems to me that the person who can create the pack that breaks down the structured archetypes by both maintaining and destroying their intrinsic representation may just be the person to tip the scales into a magically-evoked transformation of our species' behavior (it's a worthy project).

The Hierophant is, in a nutshell, religion and religiousness.

> *Religion is the masterpiece of the art of animal training, for it trains people as to how they shall think.*
>
> —ARTHUR SCHOPENHAUER (1788-1860)[1]

> *Give me a child until he is seven and I will give you the man.*
>
> —A JESUIT PROVERB ATTRIBUTED TO FRANCIS XAVIER[2]

The human animal has a definite leaning toward spirituality, and awareness of wonder, as a seeming aspect of our intrinsic nature, but the problem of religion is people—their invention of rules, protocol, dogma, creed, doctrine, law, morality, and the need, throughout history, to force these things onto others.

Earlier packs of Tarot called the Hierophant *"The Pope,"* attesting to the fact that the Roman Church influenced, even as it condemned, this very un-Christian tool of divination. The image and title of the card was changed by later occultists to represent the more supposedly mystical ideal of Greek mythological authority: the High Priest.

The child is now at the stage within the cycle of the influence of contemporary religion: dualism. Good and bad (or good and evil) are common euphemisms, as are right and wrong. The ideas of reward and punishment are introduced, as are the detestable hierarchical concepts of lofty and base (greater-than and lesser-than), conditioning intrinsic bigotries into consciousness. Morality based on the above becomes entrenched. At the same time the *ideal* of religion may also be introduced and, if that were all, then the reintroduction of the ways

---

1 Source—http://en.thinkexist.com/quotes/arthur_schopenhauer/
2 Source—http://en.wikipedia.org

of the High Priestess card would soften the effects of both the Emperor and the Hierophant but this is rare to my knowledge as, among humans, there is always hierarchy[3] with a supreme deity (almost universally male) at the top.

The child becomes an adolescent and *The Lovers*—the card that, among other things, represents *choice*, begins its work on the psyche. A time of questioning and often rebellion against the principles of the previous two cards is stimulated by changing hormones and as a reaction against the power of others over the person's individuality. It is a time when decisions regarding who one is to become in one's own future are as potent as awakened sexuality; where we stand at the crossroads of consensual success or failure and where the drive to compete and succeed (in whatever undertaking) becomes the dominating urge. It is when we look at others often as archetypes that we either dismiss them as inappropriate to the image we choose to present to the world or, through admiration, seek to mirror.

Traditionally, crossroads are dangerous places, and choices made now are likely to have an impact for many years to come. All over the world one will find folk tales and superstitions of fairies, goblins, ghosts, and daemons residing at desolate crossroads awaiting the weary traveler. These junctions became common burial sites for suicides and murderers. On many occasions, the superstition ran so deep that sacrifices were made at crossroads to ward off the evil spirits that lurked there, so that for the adolescent there is always turmoil at every level of consciousness.

The Chariot gets them through whatever gauntlet the Lovers has had them run. It represents victory, but never without striving and effort.

Whether the individual passes the tests and exams required of them by the systems of education within their cultural framework; whether they transcend the challenges of indigenous adulthood ceremony; or whether, through a choice made to turn one's back on consensual authority, and the standards set by society as measuring success, each person will experience this card *in some fashion* and the victory is always reflected through others' acclaim; is always both recognized by the individual and applauded by others.

The individual is still in their teen years.

---

[3] This is true for many other species also, but differs in the extension into concepts of divinity.

The *Strength* card is the time when we seek to imprint ourselves on culture, peer group, or field of endeavor. It is said to be a time of deepening but it is also a time when we either learn to control urges that surfaced during adolescence or give them reign and use them to dominate, repress, or subdue others. It is still a time of testing and challenge, one that will not cease for many, many years in the average lifespan of any person. The challenge is *how* we behave within our struggle for independence and self-sufficiency; within our struggle for the respect of others, the physical tools and skills we acquire; the bodies we inhabit and how we treat them.

The Strength card is a time when many seek to fit into traditional roles determined by whatever is currently acceptable or popular in society, and complacency can settle in, becoming a pattern that will, ultimately, be destroyed in one way or another, simply because it is in the nature of a cycle.

And still the individual is in their teen years.

Ah! *The Hermit* card! One of the meanings of this card is aloneness.

When was it that you secretly and fearfully, within the depths of yourself, wondered if it was your destiny to be alone or lonely? Everyone of whom I have ever asked this question has assured me that they have felt this, and that they had needed to suppress the thought as soon as it arose just in case—a strange superstition. Well, the Hermit card assures you that you will have this experience at least once; no matter how many people are around you, no matter how few.

Some will seek it willingly and their challenge is to find the space for that aloneness because the sure thing about aloneness is that it is not loneliness—a very different thing. For there to be balance and wholeness within the self those times when we are alone are integral to deep thinking and to the gaining of wisdom from the experiences and knowledge of living.

Others have isolation thrust upon them through circumstances and their challenge is to seek meaning throughout this time and to come to a place of peace while waiting to pass through it. My mind wanders, as I write, to Nelson Mandela, imprisoned for twenty-four years, and his wife Winnie who, in 1969, was imprisoned and kept in solitary confinement for seventeen months! What must they have thought? What kind of torture is it to feel no tenderness, to have no real interaction with anyone for extended periods?

At its depths, the challenge of the Hermit card is soul-searching, and on the Soul's Journey this can occur at any age and many times within one lifetime, but never more so than throughout the teenage years.

The *Wheel of Fortune* can very often represent "Groundhog Day," or the tedium of routine tasks. "I'm bored!" is the catchphrase that every parent dreads hearing from the lips of their offspring, along with "I'm too tired," or "I can't . . ." There's really nothing else to say about the Wheel of Fortune at this point. It's whatever treadmill the person treads, and the individual who is still under the care and supervision of an authority—be it parent or state—and all that this implies.

The Chayoth ha-Qadesh (four holy living creatures) at each of the corners of this card in traditional packs is there to remind us that no matter how routine or relentless our day-to-day existence might seem, there is always a beyond; a next thing.

The *Justice* card—on the Soul's Journey the individual moves into the time of being "legal". This is the transition from teens into the twenties, when the person can obtain a car license and sign a legal document; a time when many things previously out of reach become possible. It can be a time of liberation, but not without its pitfalls. Unless one comes from a highly affluent family that provides them with their every whim, it is also a time when many, many people take the leap into debt: credit card, personal loan for a car, tenancy agreement, or mortgage. Work contracts are signed by some while others enter into marriage. Higher education fees have to be found; passports acquired for travel. It is a very fine line that the individual walks here and many are still too young to see the danger!

It is a time of being judged and of judging, and discernment is the challenge. Shackles await the outcome to unclear choices—shackles that may take years to throw off.

The Second Phase—"Dropping from the Parent Tree": INDIVIDUATION
The Seed or Chrysalis
For each and every child who takes the Soul's Journey into what we term adulthood The *Hanged Man* is the precursor to the second phase of the cycle. It is when the individual, who began the cycle of challenge at the cliff-top with the Fool card, drops, lets go, or is pushed over the edge.

This is a form of living death, necessary for life to continue.

The analogy for the entire process is based on the symbol of the tree: the first phase of our lives is suffused with all the structures of culture, family, society, tradition, religion, expectation and, except in rare cases where the cycle varies considerably from the norm, predictably similar to one's forebears through lack of a recognizable alternative. Therefore we are said to be our parent tree.

The second phase, from the Hanged Man onward, is when that tree fruits, the fruit drops to the ground and seems to rot, but is, in actuality, the placenta for the as-yet-unopened seed of a new tree, which is the individual released from the tree within which it formed. It can never be the same tree thereafter, despite it being the same species. The same could be said for the passage of the ages and for every task ever undertaken, every relationship ever experienced.

The time of the Hanged Man is like the second phase of the Fool card—it could be an almost imperceptible event or a single word spoken just as easily as serious illness or loss. Either way the effects will be catastrophic and everything that we have previously relied upon as solid ground is no longer there to support us.

The Hanged Man, in this fashion, is the herald of the Dark Night of the Soul—the Saturn Return, which occurs between the ages of twenty-seven and thirty years old.

The Dark Night of the Soul

Please be aware that even though the following cards may occur as separate events, they are intrinsically linked as one experience.

The *Death* card follows. It leads you to the maw of all that you have taken for granted and asks the question "Who are you?" Should you answer with what you've always presumed to be the truth without questioning *everything* about the way you live and what you most value? Then death in life is the inevitable outcome. You will have fallen onto concrete that will take its own season to break down and that may happen in another approximately twenty-eight years, or not come at all in the person's current body.

If you *do* question (and the driving force to do so is often overwhelming) and you change in accord with the depths into which you dive, then you will have fallen onto fertile soil and the chances of the seed that you have been reduced to cracking open to reveal the wonder of who you are destined to become will begin the journey of revelation.

The *Temperance* card is a form of alchemy. I describe it to students in two ways. The first is the analogy of a tightrope walker, walking a wire strung between one cliff (Chokmah, where the Fool awaits the fall) and another (where it also waits on the cliff-edge of Binah) with only a long staff,[4] to balance and counter-balance, between the self and certain destruction at the base of the vast abyss below. During the Dark Night of the Soul one must be wary of the word "too" because it imposes untenable limitations: too old, too young, too late, too tired, too difficult, too . . . anything, will tip the staff too far. Temperance is about patience; being kind to yourself during the transition; being honest.

The other analogy is the alchemy of baking bread. To do this, many things must happen. The grain must be cut and winnowed and ground to flour; it must be mixed with ingredients that are other than it, and kneaded and kneaded until the separate parts are no longer separate; then it is left to rise, only to be punched flat and left to rise again. This being done, it is shoved into an oven, and the intense heat of the fire transforms it right down to the molecular level. When it is released from this state it is left to cool and is consumed. This is you. This is the process of transformation. This is also why change is intrinsically feared, because there is always a Dark Night of the Soul.

The Devil card (whose planetary association is Saturnian—being Capricorn) is the doubt; the threat of what you could lose; the savage forest; the labyrinthine maze where you seem to be lost and where you are sure there is a pattern—a formula for making it to the centre or the outside—that eludes you. It represents what you think you cannot get out of and what you fear, fear, fear—the temptation to try to remain who you were. You can try, but it will be an illusion—a shallow thing—and you will know, no matter what you pretend.

And I will not for one moment suggest that the threats around this time are symbolic only because that would be a lie. But the very cool thing about fear is that it is never an enemy—it is your instinct to respond to threat and heeding it is always wise, but only when the threat is real. The Devil card, at this time of life, is the illusory threat of the unknown.

The Tower, Lightning-Struck Tower, or *Blasted Tower* occurs, again, all roiled up within the turbulence of this progression. It is as though you are a deep-sea submersible and you have reached the very depths of the ocean floor, only to find that you are, in actuality, on a shelf; on the brink of a drop into yet another abyss. It is where everything seems to fall to

---

4 This is a reference to the Ace of Wands, which is, simplistically, linked to the art of communication.

pieces or explode. Your adrenals are on overdrive and your gut is responding so strongly to circumstances that your hands shake and your palms sweat and your legs are barely able to support you. Been there? If you have passed your Saturn Return you're remembering right now exactly what we're talking about.

The Medieval Tarot deck, the Tarot of Marseille—called the Blasted Tower, *La Maison Dieu*, the House of God, with all the ramifications of the Tower of Babel and the biblical curse for the hubris of causing all people to speak in different languages so that they could no longer understand one another—a very stupid curse, if you ask me, but it is apt to our purpose here because, as is certain, two or more people could seem to be speaking even the same language and yet misunderstand each other.

On a relationship level, whether that is a couple living together, a family, a community, or a nation, the Tower is the result of misunderstandings that lead to the breakdown of peace and the resulting explosion of aggression.

During this time the Blasted Tower will express itself in countless varieties of tragedy or confrontation, but the one thing about being blown from our ivory towers of treasured illusion is that once we hit bottom we can fall no further, and if we survive the fall then we must move on.

The other name of the Tower card—the Lightning Struck Tower—is a direct analogy of the "fall from the parent tree," the natural state of the transition from Kether to Malkuth, in the direction of the Lightning Flash in its continuous evolution.
It is the process of the seed cracking open.

Redemption and Transition
The Star card—As of 2006 CE science is coming closer and closer to mapping the human genome, the supposed blueprint to life. The more fascinating question, though, still remains: what is it that defines life in difference to matter? What is it that endows us with emotion? What is the *quality* of individualism? These questions are inherent within the process of the Soul's Journey; they are represented by the Star card insofar as no matter how much we learn there is always the universe's next trick, but the Star card encourages us to reach toward the surface again after the long deep night of the soul. It is the person released from the confines of the shell of the seed. We are vulnerable, sure, but . . . the Star card also reminds us that we are now certain of our place within the scheme of forever and that by being ourselves, rather than mimicking others, we will attract people and events aligned with us. It is like the Magician card at the beginning of the first phase, just with more vision.

I'm taking more time with *The Moon* card than any other card because of its implications. First of all it is comparable, on this journey, with the High Priestess card (which has the Moon as its associated planetary body) and at first there may be a lack of clear steps of progress and we see only "through a glass but darkly"; a veil, but now we are beyond the curtains and out by the water. The image on the card itself displays a crustacean, a dog, and a wolf—all arcs of seeming progression on an evolutionary scale, but is that the truth when all three creatures exist now? No. What the image really projects is that we are all connected; are creatures of Oceania—Earth's womb—whether submerged or on dry land, and the Moon and the waters remind us of our commonality, while the path lures us toward a future unknown.

The Moon card is inherently moist reminding the person that, on the journey of the seed to becoming a tree, nourishment comes from the element of water which, in people, is how we emote and the way we feel.

It is instinct and intuition rather than rationale and logic, but that doesn't mean it isn't about thinking, because so many people are ruled by their emotions—their desires, expectations, anxieties, ambitions, what others think, conceptual fears as well as real ones—that life for many can be made up of illusions of past and future and traps of need. At the Moon card point in life, the individual is required to delve into their emotional attachment to past and current experience, mental state, and the quality of what is thought and felt. These are survival tools. It is important for the person to see the ways that they or others use emotion as a chess game of manipulation or blackmail and to get right off the board by self-reflection and reflection on their relationships with others, by processing the information and transforming it all into a quality experience.

People are manipulated and assaulted from every direction by jargon and implication—mostly repetition; mostly rhetoric.

At the end of an Aikido class a few years ago all the students were seated on the mats. The fellow who had taken the class in the head sensei's absence talked to the practitioners for a while, about what he'd been taught regarding people; about the conscious and subconscious mind. He informed us that the subconscious was white, or positive, and that if we had negative thoughts (black) they would go into the subconscious and turn it grey.

The concept was ridiculous.

Dualisms like good/bad, black/white, and positive/negative merely reinforce the stereotypical paradigms that have become a religious and political tool—as well as a major advertising ploy—for manipulating people into an untrue view of what is acceptable or otherwise. It seems like it's been done forever. These concepts are just that: concepts. They have no reference to life.

So what's the reality?

The dissolution of androcentric thought is how one breaks through from being seed to individual plant; an absolution from thinking humanly to the denial of everything else, except, perhaps, peripherally.

Analogy

Not far from where I live there is a place called Protestors Falls.

At the end of a track that meanders through the rainforest is a deep pool, fed from a waterfall that cascades down a 240-foot escarpment. It can be quite loud there beside the pool, sitting upon boulders that embrace it, because the place is a natural amphitheatre. Bat caves exist high up in the cliff face; ferns and native plants grow in profusion, defying gravity from rocky outcroppings.

Sitting there, you can look up toward the top of the falls. The experience is akin to reverse vertigo. The sky sits above it all in such a vivid blue as to hurt the eyes. Birds whip-call across the valley.

I've been there as dusk turns to dark and the profusion of fireflies warp the senses in the darkness as they flicker between huge trees and land on my eyelashes.

The place is holy.

The water from the falls comes from elsewhere—higher up—from among the gorges and gullies, catchments for rain and spring-fed creeks.

It thunders or trickles, depending on the season, into the deep pool at its base, it murmurs and tumbles down and down, over rock and rock and rock, linking with other creeks and waterways until it reaches the sea.

Of course.

But along the journey of its destiny are habitats. Frogs live there: lizards, birds, snakes, echidna, wallabies, turtles, and, so I have been told, platypus. They have lived around or in the waters of this place from the Dreamtime.

But tour buses sometimes bring people from far away, and isn't it nice to take a dip in the deep, deep pure waters of the pool at the base of the falls?

They are responsible for the decimation of these habitats; for the poisoning of these waters. They wear deodorant, perfume, sun-block, make-up, hair product; false things; toxic things.

And if someone just told them to be clean of all these things first? To enter the waters aware?

The subconscious is not a void, nor is it a mess. It can be a garden or a forest of wild profusion—that depends on the *nature* of a person, and it doesn't matter which—but each mind is unique and will flourish as long as it remains in its natural state. We must be very careful to prevent that which is toxic, or noxious, or alien, from gaining hold.

To do this requires a modicum of detachment: from emotional detachment to material; from 'buying into' the jargon or the expectations of others; from outside interference that seeks to tell you what is right or wrong, black or white, positive or negative.

A mind like clear water takes care. It requires love and it needs to be left alone sometimes. To be quiet.

Your body will usually inform you of when you are being pressured or polluted by unnatural things. It will suffer agitation or tension; your gut will express anxiety; your head will experience pressure, maybe your hands will shake. Perhaps you will suffer want, and this will cause confusion and sometimes even despair. Maybe you won't sleep so well anymore.

Let it go. Take it off yourself. Fix it.

I've swum in that pool at the base of Protestors Falls, naked and clean. I've straddled what I call The God Rock, in the heart of the waters. I've been there for solstice and equinox.

It taught me: Have a mind like what I am, it said, like clear water.

The Sun card is the new birth. It is the person who has broken free of the seed's confines and has begun to put down roots and spread and reach out into life independent of all that has gone before. It's exactly like being born again and is the next revolution of the Magician card. Some will never experience this. Those who do know what really living is all about, no matter the experiences, live for the *sake* of living. Everything can be handled when the person comes to this understanding. It is freedom despite the circumstances. It is the knowledge that all things are destiny but each of us has a choice as to how we *respond* to all things.

The *Judgement* card is, ultimately, this rebirth, but it is also the moment in life when everything is changed and will continue changing, when the life that began with the Sun card becomes affected by the person's *unique* experience of wind, rain, sun, and snow (work, family, friendships, hardships), and *knowing* that there is free will involved in the choices made in response to everything that happens also implies wisdom.

The World is everything that happens in the new cycle until the next death and cycle, and the one after that and the one after that (infinitely). It is when the person has secured themselves within the new cycle and their roots are strong enough to hold them steady no matter the weather or conditions. The Chayoth Ha-Qadesh (the four holy living creatures) stand in the corners of most traditional Tarot packs, as they do with the Wheel of Fortune, and the objects upon the altar of the Magician card, both as symbol and object, represent this—reminding us, again, that there is *more*, again, beyond what we consider; there is and will always be more.

Practice: Where Am I Now?

To find out where you or someone else is, in what is likely to be simply one of many cycles within one's lifetime, you will use all the cards.

Shuffle them and lay them out in as shown in figure 12: a clockwise circle with 11 cards forming the upper arc and 11 forming the lower.

In this case the positioning of the cards in the Unit 7 theory section will reflect where the individual is right now in their current cycle.

To gauge where you or the individual is *right now* you are to look at the traditional position of the Fool card and the two or three that follow it around the circle and contemplate the meaning, as one card is not sufficient to give an understanding of progression. It is more than likely that you or the person in your group is part way through a cycle and the cards themselves will tell you where. For example:

- The Knight of Pentacles or the Knight of Cups falls where the Chariot card does in the traditional circle—this indicates that tests or exams one has passed in the past are progressing well either practically or to one's satisfaction.
- The Queen of Wands falls where the Moon card traditionally falls—this indicates a woman (if not oneself or one's study companion) who is perhaps going through an emotionally difficult or disillusioning time that will affect who is being read for.

- The 10 of Cups falls where the Judgement card traditionally falls—this indicates changes to or in the home or family.

These are all blatant and easy examples and it will not always be so, but when you see something similar that is as easily recognizable as this, and the event has already occurred, you can then glean the current phase of the cycle and get an understanding of the *effects* that will follow (in difference to events).

UNIT EIGHT

The 78 Cards and Their Meanings

Theory: The Major Arcana—Meanings

Please note: there are many other meanings to this stuff. It all depends on the moment, who one is reading for, what the pattern of several cards looks like, and many other factors. You do need to learn the following, though, and very well. Just don't be so rigid as to insist interpretations have only these meanings, as these meanings are given to you as examples based on both experience and the psychic color of the card . . . and that will *always* depend on what it falls with!

For multiple card meanings on all the following please reference the Appendix.

0—The Fool

The Fool card is also known as the blind card, because it will very rarely allow you to know what it is saying. There is a purpose in this: in certain instances in our lives an event is *so* important that the trigger (The Fool) must remain unknown to ensure that, no matter the consequences, these events occur without preconceptions.

It can represent a seemingly random, or trickster, event; it can be something seemingly stupid that will engender unforeseen repercussions.

It can be the client walking down the street and bumping into a stranger who becomes integral to their life and it also suggests that the client could be about to do something very rash that will have all kinds of unexpected consequences.

Life will change as a direct result of being touched by the Fool.

You can never guess what it might engender because you'd be wrong. You'll only know its importance retrospectively—it can seem like an innocuous event, completely irrelevant, hence the idea of blindly stepping off a cliff by seeming accident.

Nothing that shows up after this card is recognizable from the current perspective—it is the ultimate universe's next trick and it *is* Destiny; exposed and pre-determined.

1—The Magician

A whole new event or way of life is about to unfold when this card appears, but with knowledge and learning preceding the change.

The Magician card can represent a person or a people who do not like to be told what to do or that operate independently from traditional roles, and as such it can represent a very powerful individual or group.

It can be a magical practitioner (even a stage magician if professional cards attend it) or the path of that person; a specialist in anything and one who has achievements academically or in a specific field; a learned person—one with qualifications.

2—The Priestess

This card represents that which is mysterious, hidden, sacred, or behind the scenes; anything not seen, occult situations, a sacred way of the mysteries. As a place it can represent homes or environments that are hidden from general view or that traditionally represent sacredness.

Secrecy; client confidentiality (as in a lawyer, doctor, priest, psychic) and can represent a priestess or practitioner of the occult arts and the qualities of an individual if he or she is psychic or empathic.

This card can mean there is something hidden that can sometimes come to light; things going on behind the scenes.

It can also be an article that becomes lost, hidden, or missing, that the client won't be able to find and can represent an event that will have no answer (like whether another is being "unfaithful" in the traditional sense).

The High Priestess card can also represent a veil in more than one sense—it can be literally a bridal veil, a hijab, or a burqa, and this card can often describe places that the client will visit.

3—The Empress

She is all that is beautiful (or considered beautiful, which is a different thing and can be quite dangerous, like the cruel tradition of bound feet), sensual, artistic, tactile, and female.

The card can represent hospitality or the hospitality industry, industries catering to the consensual idea of beauty: from the fashion industry through cosmetics, even cosmetic surgery.

It is fecundity, pregnancy of any kind from biological to the conception of a project or artistic endeavor. Biologically it represents the womb or breasts.

In the cycle of the seasonal year it is both when the produce is ripe and juicy and also when the land is ready for planting.

It can be any juicy thing, from fruit to gossip to sexuality.

When shown as a place, the climate is always tropical but it can just as easily represent one's ancestral or mother lands; places of moisture, not wetness.

It is nurturing; motherhood; pregnancy; and procreation.

4—The Emperor

This card represents that which is patriarchal or orthodox. It can mean fatherhood and what that traditionally entails. It can also represent a politician, a president, or a prime minister.

It can be talking about authority bodies: insurance, banks, administration, and establishments such as educational systems, hospitals, and government.

It very often shows itself when associated with traditional learning in difference to private study interests.

This particular card is more often than not accompanied by others that will give it deeper significance, as will its placing within a spread.

5—The Hierophant

In most instances the Hierophant has religious connotations and, in some ways, always represents these institutions, even in places such as Adelaide (called the city of churches) or traditionally Roman Catholic or Islamic countries, but I have not seen it represent Jewish, Buddhist, or Hindu lands.

It represents everything from dogmatic, structured, hierarchical religions to New Age spirituality that resembles traditional religion, and it can also be a person who is a religious or spiritual figurehead in the public eye: traditional, orthodox, or otherwise.

It is marriage—whether traditionally religious, a couple living together in a loving partnership, or the marriage of businesses and corporations.

6—The Lovers

The ultimate meaning of this card is choice, but it can also represent split decisions, division of any kind, three-way relationships, or triangular relationships (of the sexual kind). In the physical body it can represent the lungs, hips, or pelvis.

The Lovers represents "choice" as an outcome; Tarot will not give a direct answer because there is free will involved in a decision.

The card can also be that there will be multiple outcomes and it can also show a crossroads in a person's life.

As an answer to a question it indicates that the client will have more than one choice and Tarot is not answering because it does not want to influence the individual's decision.

It can also represent children who are twins.

7—The Chariot

If we are talking about individuals, this card represents victory after striving: a pass (exams, driving test, medical checkup) or any personal sense of achievement whereas it can also represent places or modes of transportation.

The Chariot indicates acceptance after a job interview; the winning of a court case; the winning of any battle, dispute, or war, and it represents an earned victory with hard work before and after.

This card can also simply be read as winning—anything from a lottery to horse-racing—but the context would apply in a spread of several cards.

It is very malleable and deceptive when describing a person—you'd need context: the person could be a very great ally or an enemy who beats you.

It also relates to certain places and interests, very often associated with Middle-Eastern lands, past and present.

8—Strength

The Strength card can be the physical body, control issues, infections due to erupt, seismic areas, foundations poured for a building, an animal, or bodywork of any kind.

This card will turn up in many environment spreads and can be a desert anywhere.

The Strength card also lends power to other cards.

It can represent animals, lust, underground or under-the-surface power, and rage, depending on other cards.

When representing a person, this card insures good health and physical prowess, and it will describe many physical activities and attributes.

9—The Hermit

The Hermit is aloneness, but not sadness or loneliness unless other cards indicate; it can be an unattached person, a wise person, an old or elderly person.

Environmentally, it is a hilly or mountainous place, a cold country or wintry place.

The card can represent antiques and antique dealers, or those people or things that relate to old or ancient things.

Architecturally it is old houses, gabled houses, chalets, or homes with height.

Environmentally it is places outside cities, high places, or many variations (see Appendix).

Sometimes it represents a quest or a vigil.

10—Wheel of Fortune

This card suggests motion, backward and forward, over and over, up and down, a roller-coaster ride, the daily round, day to day, continuous.

It can represent a circuit (at a gym, or someone who does a market circuit) but I have also had it appear in readings for people who are involved with a circus.

It can literally represent the wheels of a vehicle and can be the routine or cyclical maintenance of anything.

Very often there is a sense of simple routine or sameness. This, for some clients, can be disconcerting (depending on the situation), whereas for others it is comforting.

11—Justice

Justice is a loaded word with many meanings and can represent any legal matter from the judicial system to contracts, leases, legalities, the police, the courts, anything whereby you sign on the dotted line.

It also, however, signifies discernment and could mean that the client will be required to make selective decisions.

The Justice card can represent anything from a person who works in the legal field to one who is called up for jury duty. It all depends on other attending cards in the layout.

12—Hanged Man

This can be descriptive, in one way or another, of a person. It can be a martyr in the dysfunctional sense; putting up with discord or a distressing situation out of fear of change; being a doormat in a relationship; or in the spiritual or visionary sense: people like Nelson Mandela and Gandhi.

One of the catchphrases of this card is to "consider the experience an exercise in detachment."

This card can represent falling, being rejected, suicide, a thing or person becoming obsolete; humanitarianism, altruism, genuine spirituality.

This card, in many senses, represents a situation (similar to The Fool card) where things are beyond one's control.

13—Death

This card represents completion; a relationship or undertaking is over; it is the end of a venture; a full stop. The Death card always represents very real endings and can be very exciting or very tragic.

It literally means "No" if, during question time, the first card on the table in a yes/no question is the Death card. No other cards are to be necessarily laid out when this occurs.

In situations of study it will represent the final exams, and cards surrounding it will tell of success or failure. It also means literal death, but that is not always a disturbing thing. On a seasonal level, for example, it will represent harvest. On a festive note, it can be Samhain: Hallow'een, or in Mexico, the Day of the Dead.

I have seen it celebrated and mourned, depending on the background/lifestyle of the situation. If, for example, a person dies at a very old age, Tarot tends to view it as a celebration of the individual's life rather than something sad and, as such, the client will actually hear words along these lines at the funeral.

It can also indicate places of violent deaths. I recall seeing the Death card with the Empress card and the Universe/World card in the reading of a traveler: it indicated Cambodia which, under the Khmer Rouge, was known as the Killing Fields. You would see similar appearances in other lands bathed in a history of bloodshed. An interesting and hitherto unique layout foretold the September 11 World Trade Center deaths.

14—Temperance

This is the alchemy of mixing one thing with another to get something else; the "I'm not there yet" tightrope walker (and their balancing stick); cautions; all things worthy of consideration; trial period; a middle position: mediation, negotiation, careful peace (treaty), walking a fine line through a particular situation, keeping your balance, someone on the wagon (drugs or alcohol).

It can be a person who is "piggy in the middle" in a situation of discord, and it will represent mediators, mellow people, counselors, and healers.

In the entertainment industry it represents balancing acts, jugglers, tightrope or high-wire acts. It represents balancing life without overindulgences, and when describing places it can represent bridges.

In a Tree of Life spread, when falling in Kether, it represents a profound peace.

15—The Horned One (The Devil)

This card represents fear. There is a definite threat (in the mind and/or literally) forthcoming; it can represent an addiction (alcohol, drugs, food, sex, even the need to be loved), but it can also represent an enemy, particularly if it describes someone. With ill-health cards it can represent cancer, a sexually transmitted disease, but it can also represent being stuck, obsession, dogma, or danger. It can represent people or institutions that have radical, fundamentalist, or dangerous ideologies.

In a place it can mean claustrophobic conditions or confined spaces, it can be frustration over delays, restraints, or restrictions.

The Devil card has a disproportionate number of interpretations (see Appendix) depending on its placement within a spread, informing us of prevalence toward dysfunction and danger in our current world.

In the Llewellyn pack we can transcend the monotheist overtones that denote "evil" and also perceive this card as an invitation to question what we are often demanded we fear. What, after all, denotes wildness? Who defines "evil"?

16—The Tower

In a spread this card can inform us that things are about to go terribly wrong. Here is where what the person (or situation) presumed to be secure comes tumbling down; chaos, fiery places, people to do with mining, explosive situations of any kind. Natural phenomena include lightning, big storms, cyclones, eruptions, and earthquakes. It can also be electricity but dangerously uncontained power.

Up it blows, down it goes. Crisis; out-of-control events and people. Rage. Whatever has been built up will come crashing down.

This card will show up as anything from a war, or the downfall of a government or corporation, to an emergency worker.

The Tower, in personal or cultural situations, is a dramatic precursor to change and, as such, can ultimately be liberating.

17—The Star

Pandora's box is still left with Hope after the ills of the Universe are released, being beyond discord. The Hebrew letter associated with this card is Heh (window) allowing us to see clearly to the other side, head above water, to see greatness in the smallest.

The Star can represent flight and aeronautics, long distance/time/long-term projects, realization.

This card can indicate a definite "Yes" in answer to a question.

It also represents illumination, cameras, film, IT and other forms of technology; glass, shop-fronts; advertising, visual imagery, reflection, ideals, and information.

It also represents many places, depending on with which other cards it falls, and can give quite precise time durations—usually of many years: seventeen to twenty, for instance.

18—The Moon

Deceit or self-deceit, disillusionment, disappointment, wet places, a moody person, depression, the mind, a situation or person that is emotionally wet, miserable.

The Moon card can also represent the ocean and all things to do with wet weather, flooding, or water of any kind; things that descend—divers, fishermen; also any pastime that is oceanic or involving water.

Physiologically, the Moon card can represent being affected by dreary weather such as by SAD (seasonal affective disorder); it can represent hormonal shifts or imbalances. It represents the persona or image of an individual; or can simply represent reflection or a mirror.

It will also show up when dealing with art or image-related situations.

19—The Sun

This card is basically a representation of success, achievement, birth, children, hot places, or anything bright or golden.

The Sun card is very innocent and full of joy and happiness. It represents the beginning of things as easily as it represents outcomes. Mostly its meaning, like all other cards, is dependent on those cards around it. It is not necessary for anything more to be said.

20—Judgement

This card represents all forms of change: usually major change in one's life style, progress, rebirth, change of circumstances, changes of mind, change, change, change; initiations of any kind.

It also represents awakenings, or reawakenings, and times of advancement and liberation from that which has caused restriction and constraint.

21—The Universe (The World)

This card represents the world itself, community, overseas connections, the end of one cycle and the beginning of another like 31 December to 1 January, or like Samhain on the witch's calendar, and it can also represent the cycle of one year, any seasonal cycle, even one's entire biological life's journey.

It can also represent twenty to twenty-one years ago or into the future, a Saturn Cycle; the transition from one way of living to another.

It can also represent planetary and astrological associations.

The Minor Arcana—Meanings

Please note: the Knights are rarely (if ever) people.

Wands

They relate to communications, the spoken and the written word, the performing arts, spontaneity, creativity, self-expression.

Ace of Wands

New beginnings, creative works—more casual than intense; new beginnings that, like the Magician Card, are spontaneous and seemingly more naturally occurring.

This card represents the words "new" and "yes." It can literally represent fire or a fiery situation, spontaneity, or excitation.

It is books and all forms of communication, both spoken and written. It can be new possessions and objects.

It is light-heartedness, vivacity, dance, optimism, and never represents a problem.

2 of Wands

In difference to many other cards, the 2 of Wands does not represent events so much as environments within which the client will find themselves, and in this instance it is a coastal place, usually a large or a major city. If it is a smaller place such as a seaside village, the cards around it will advise. In the Appendix you will find several instances of place, but your intuition will necessitate the interpretation.

The only instance where it represents other than this is when it describes a person, and in this it represents an individual who is very affluent, with nothing to prove.

3 of Wands

"At a distance": this is a place card and all its associations are in the Appendix.

It can also represent time sequences: a period of three days, three weeks, three months, or three years.

4 of Wands

A party, festival, or celebration; a good time; a performance. With a person card it describes the individual as a living celebration or a performer.

This card displays theatrical events and can even represent restaurants and the hospitality industry.

5 of Wands

This card can indicate confusion of thought; many voices at once; a band or group of singers; or it can represent several people talking or interacting at once. It can be a literal mess: people, room, and/or environment; doing several things at once; building materials; verbal dispute; red tape.

On another level it can also literally represent people fighting with sticks and stones, not tanks and guns, but you will usually find it in political or politically-derived situations, often when Tarot interrupts a reading to tell of world events.

6 of Wands

Natural victory, another "Yes" card; cruising easy; nothing stressful; easily victorious; natural achievement; slide on through. There are no specific this-goes-with-that to be aware of here. With this card present, the spread indicates that by being who your client, the person, or the situation is *naturally* (without pretension for any reason), events will unfold without stress or duress.

7 of Wands

This card can represent telephone calls or internet chat; teaching; internal conversations with oneself.

When in reference to the sale of a house or property it represents an auction; long-distance speaking—not eye to eye; talking where not everyone is listening.

I have also had this card turn up when communication occurred from so-called dead people who are still around the client and attempting to communicate, and also when the Mysteries are in communication with an individual, which will normally occur accompanied by the High Priestess card.

8 of Wands

Rural land or country but not necessarily forested; sending out things (documents or other forms of written material).

9 of Wands

Not being heard, or not speaking—"Nobody ever listens to me." The client or represented person is annoyed at people finishing their sentences; the person is not going to waste time explaining themselves; not wasting words; communication breakdown. In the warning spread it means to keep your mouth shut. The person has had enough of not being listened to and is guarding his or her words. This is the person who would rather communicate, but it's pointless—not going to do that anymore.

10 of Wands

This can mean moving things from place to place; shouldering responsibilities willingly; can be building.

It is never a hardship.

Knight of Wands

The Knights are rarely, if ever, a representation of people, but of movements such as a journey, trip, communication, package, or letter. There is usually nothing insidious or worrying when this card is involved.

It represents modes of transport—usually an average car—and it also represents an amicable resolution to a situation.

Page of Wands

Fire-sign children/child of a fire-sign person; the seed of a creative project; the spoken or the written word; a small fiery thing.

It can also represent a book, journal, or treatise.

Queen of Wands

A fire-sign woman; out there, active, in-your-face people; highly communicative; women with red hair (natural or otherwise) and/or freckles, or it can be someone with a ruddy complexion.

King of Wands

A fire-sign man; out there, active, in-your-face people; highly communicative; men with red hair (natural or otherwise) or red in their beard, and/or freckles, or it can be someone with a ruddy complexion.

Cups
Emotional, Artistic, Emissive

Ace of Cups

Love without any definitions; a feeling; the roots of the powers of love; a state of love with another person but the other person is irrelevant; one's own personal Holy Grail.

2 of Cups

This card always represents intimate relationships, often (mostly) sexual but can also mean very close friendships. Mostly it's just sex and/or sexuality.

3 of Cups

A gathering of like-minded people; small group of people getting along well; the quality of a gathering; communion stronger than blood; no disharmony; three people.

It can also represent a reunion and you will find this when it appears in conjunction with major events such as religious festivals, marriages, and funerals.

4 of Cups

This card represents other than what the person is looking for or at. It indicates that events will happen unexpectedly; it can be a gift, an offer, or an unforeseen opportunity, and in the case of the prospective sale of a home or property it can represent an offer other than what is first presented.

It informs the client that there will be more options open to them in any situation present in the spread.

It shows a person, seemingly content with what they care about or have, who has pleasant and unconsidered surprises yet to come.

It is not always propitious, however, and if there are cards of detriment in the spread it will indicate unforeseen consequences.

5 of Cups

This is a card of sadness or regret. It can represent mourning for a loss, either through death or separation; a backward-looking person—someone concerned with past losses or disappointments; a person so concerned with what has failed they do not seek alternatives.

It can also indicate the seeking to achieve in a certain area but not getting what is wanted.

As a foundation it is a "No" card: the person won't get what they want.

It can represent a sequence of unsuccessful relationships that will not continue into the future.

6 of Cups

The past—this is ultimately what this card means, but it can also indicate children or childhood, usually reflective and often the client's own past.

It indicates that which is already gone or finished; with work cards it can represent a person involved with dead things—anything from archaeology and antiques to history and genealogy.

It will show up when there are reunions.

7 of Cups

The image of this card shows a person looking at a sequence of hopes or fears, none of which are realized.

It represents illusions; lies or a liar; little indulgences such as alcohol, sex, drugs, food, etc., but not to the point of addiction.

It can also represent the imagination when it shows itself with several Wands cards, but in detriment it is definitely delusional.

It represents "What if" situations and speculation and, as such, can be very creative because it also represents the idea that may or may not lead to an event.

8 of Cups

This card represents the process of disappointment rather than actual disappointment itself. There is hope in it because it represents *walking away* from disappointment: something vital was missing in the relationship or situation. The client or person to whom the spread relates cannot yet see where they are going but knows perfectly well where they have been.

It usually means that disappointment has already occurred, but the cup that is missing shows an innate emotional imbalance when the event is occurring.

There is definitely sadness, but it is certainly instilled with a sense of excitement or adventure.

It can mean that the Dark Night of the Soul is almost over; that someone is leaving stuff behind; that disappointment is transitional.

9 of Cups

This is called the "wish" card, and it is generally auspicious. The surrounding cards will describe the circumstances.

It is also a "Yes" card in answer to a question. The only times this card is disturbing are described in the Appendix.

10 of Cups

A house, home, or family; a place and/or state of being; somehow better than even the 9 of Cups because it is shared joy; an actual clan or a being in an environment that is one's natural habitat; where one is at peace.

Sometimes this card can represent death—a final resting or release—but only when there has been long-term illness or pain, and, even then, the Death card will be almost certain to turn up. A long time before the research and marketing of quality medications to treat HIV/AIDS began, many of the men that I read for who were suffering with this disease had the 10 of Cups as a final outcome to their suffering.

Knight of Cups

The knights are not people; they are states or modes of movement or flow. The Knight of Cups is a follow-through card: whatever is happening is honorable and can be trusted; it displays a feeling of good will; it indicates that everything is okay; it shows that the client will trust the person or persons around the card; it can signify a gift if offered, but not usually a physical object.

It can represent an offer being made or a gift being given.

Page of Cups

This can be the seed or conception of an artistic pursuit; a child born under one of the following: Cancer, Pisces, or Scorpio. It can, however, represent art, painting, drawing, sculpture, or visual arts.

With illness cards, it usually indicates a child with eye, ear, nose, or throat problems.

It can be animals, usually dark-coated.

Queen of Cups

A female water-sign person—unless accompanying cards signify that the Major Arcanum mean otherwise (see Appendix).

Can be a woman with dark hair and/or complexion; a woman who holds on to her emotions for any number of reasons.

King of Cups

A male water-sign person—unless accompanying cards signify that the Major Arcanum mean otherwise (see Appendix).

It can also represent a dark-haired or swarthy man; "the King of Hearts"; a deeply loved and loving man.

Pentacles

Practical; physical; material

Ace of Pentacles

This card represents the roots of the powers of matter; the physical body; money, finances or income coming or going; money and commodities; or the foundations of the physical world in any manner.

An interview, or impersonal discussion, always practical in nature; a craft-prson, artisan, or accomplice.

2 of Pentacles

Shared instances: divided money, shared accommodations, financial partnerships, division of possessions and/or money, part-time income or work; part-time anything.

Money; finances; securities; settlements. Financial or practical partnerships of any kind.

3 of Pentacles

An interview, or impersonal discussion, always practical in nature; a craft-person, artisan, or apprentice.

4 of Pentacles

A stay-put card; a holding-on-to card. It can represent a person or people carefully saving money; a deposit; a small stash of money; a person who doesn't or won't spend money; limited money.

In the human body it can represent: body fat; fixed joints; arthritic conditions; gall stones, kidney stones.

It can represent time sequences: four days, four weeks, four months, or four years.

Quite often shows up for any skills training or university degree, especially when accompanied by the Emperor card.

5 of Pentacles

No money; broke; poverty; lacking.

In legal settlement cases it represents a lot less money, a loss of money, or a complete loss; deficiency of something (in a health condition); overspending money.

It can be bankruptcy (of whatever kind).

I am also having a moment's chuckle because yesterday I had a client who was on crutches—her ankle broken. When the 5 of Pentacles showed itself (in my deck, depicting two people, one on crutches) in the Celtic Cross, central position crossed by the Temperance card, I burst out laughing. I picked up the card and faced her with it. She grinned and said "Oh, that's me!" Interestingly, she has been working casual rates (temporary employment) and therefore has no income while healing, hence the loss of money also represented.

6 of Pentacles

Paying out or getting paid; getting rid of a debt; being repaid money that was owed.

7 of Pentacles

Growth; the fulfillment of the growth process. It can represent increases of money, the interest on investments; productivity; savings; increases in material value as in the value of property.

It can also represent gardens, plant nurseries, roots.

8 of Pentacles

This card's ultimate meaning is work, or the word "work."

Sometimes it's a job, occupation, or vocation (although the latter would have the Ace of Cups or the 9 of Cups present); work being done on anything from a car, to a house, to a human body; what will work or won't work.

I don't need to give a this-goes-with-that here because it is simply the word: work, and can mean many things.

9 of Pentacles

The 9 of Pentacles can be best described by keywords or descriptions such as: beautiful; quality not quantity; no matter what happens life is a win-win thing; studying and learning; becoming who you are, not what you do (through life, not institutions necessarily).

Mistress or master of all they behold; no domination; a state of earthly grace.

It is the person's reputation in the world: as well as, or in difference to, the way they feel about themselves; quality in respect of whatever card it falls on or with.

10 of Pentacles

This is usually a rented or leased dwelling: a house (sometimes in difference to a home), a shop or business premises. The quality, or state, of the dwelling will depend on attending cards. Can be a studio.

Knight of Pentacles

A form of transportation: four-wheel drive, van, truck, caravan, mobile home, train, bus, etc.; ongoing practicalities; the expression "take care of business"; involvement in a process—doing the work: plod, plod.

It represents covering one's own interests; ongoing financial transactions; the movement of transactions.

Page of Pentacles

An earth-sign child (see Appendix); private study or a small personal business enterprise. Pages are time spent with kids or animals, or things you do in a small way.

Queen of Pentacles

This represents an earth-sign woman; a business woman or an earthy woman; an Anglo-Saxon, dark-haired woman.

King of Pentacles

Quite likely an earth-sign man. Can represent a business man or an earthy man; when describing a person's appearance they are an Anglo-Saxon, dark-haired person.

Swords (are always tricky things)

Intellectual; violatory; aggressive

Ace of Swords

Cutting or dividing—this is a card of willpower; of intent.

It represents decision: divisions; determination; discipline; someone in authority.

It can also depict sharp objects; chefs with knives; tattooist needles; acupuncturists; martial artists.

2 of Swords

Again, there is a list of keywords or phrases: not seen; indecision; stalemate; inward looking.

It can indicate—in a dispute—that one's back is covered.

It can inform that things are occurring behind the scenes: behind you; that there is something the individual is not seeing; that a lost object is not found; information is undisclosed.

It can also represent peace; meditation.

3 of Swords

In some way or another, this card usually represents separation. That can be anything from a marriage separation to being away from loved ones.

It is not always a problem—it can indicate when a baby comes out of the womb; a journey away from home, and missing people; homesickness.

4 of Swords

This is also a very simple-meaning card: waiting; doing nothing; nothing happening; resting.

It can represent time sequences of four days, four weeks, four months, four years, or April.

5 of Swords

Argument or dispute (somebody loses); struggle but not of the gentle kind; an argument that's going to come back at you later. Not always of detriment (see Appendix).

6 of Swords

Time sequence—six days, six weeks, six months; a journey or process out of trouble (from troubled waters to calm); on or across water close to the country in which the person lives; short journeys across water. It can also represent people and events that have to do with water.

7 of Swords

This can represent the need to be wary. It is also the card of a sneak or a cunning person. It represents avoidance of confrontation or simply avoidance; getting out of a possibly dangerous or detrimental situation "by the skin of your teeth"; can indicate a thief or theft.

It can be very propitious—the art of strategy being used in a situation that requires such.

8 of Swords

This is the "stuck" or "bound" card; inability to change: there's nothing the person can do about a situation; the person's hands are tied (sometimes literally as has been seen in the case of one individual who had achieved refugee status from an oppressive regime); limitations; fix it or forget it; nothing can be done to change the situation beyond what's already available; commitment—in it for the long run; can't move; unavoidable delays.

In answer to a question: no action.

It can also represent living along a difficult-access driveway, track, or road, or can be an injury keeping a person restrained.

9 of Swords

This card is always influenced by those around it and can be either detrimental or auspicious, depending on circumstances and even the individual's disposition.

Can be worry, regret, tiredness; fatigue; late nights; insomnia, but can just as easily signify that one works a night shift or is in the healing industry (when falling with 8 of Pentacles, for example).

When sickness is a certainty, however, this card will always turn up.

10 of Swords

Physical pain; back pain; back-stabbing; violence; cruelty and the result of cruelty; betrayal, but, as with so many other cards, can also be auspicious (see Appendix).

Knight of Swords

Speed; can also be aggression; impatience; a swift resolution to a situation.

Page of Swords

Intellect or intellectual pursuits; an air-sign child: Libra, Aquarius, Gemini.

Queen of Swords

An air-sign woman; can also be a fair-haired or grey/silver-haired, light-skinned woman; a woman of deep intelligence unless she falls with cards of detriment, whereby she becomes a woman with a cutting tongue or wit.

King of Swords

An air-sign man; may be a fair-haired or grey/silver-haired, light-skinned; a deeply intelligence man unless seen with cards of detriment, then having a cutting tongue or wit.

Time Sequences—Represented by the Pages

Page of Swords and Lovers card—the time of Gemini
Page of Swords and Star card—the time of Aquarius
Page of Swords and Justice card—the time of Libra

Page of Cups and Chariot card—the time of Cancer
Page of Cups and Death card—the time of Scorpio
Page of Cups and Moon card—the time of Pisces

Page of Pentacles and Devil card—the time of Capricorn
Page of Pentacles and Hermit card—the time of Virgo
Page of Pentacles and Hierophant card—the time of Taurus

Page of Wands and Temperance card—the time of Sagittarius
Page of Wands and Strength card—the time of Leo
Page of Wands and Emperor card—the time of Aries

Part Three
Practicing Your Craft

UNIT NINE

The First Nine Months

Preparation

Studying the preceding units will have, by this stage of the training, lubed your psyche and consciousness like oil on a rusty hinge, and you are ready now to experiment with the practicalities and later, in Units 6 and 9, there are complete readings for you to work with.

If you have not done so already, now is the time to go out and purchase your Tarot pack. It is ultimately your choice which deck you go with, but for the time being I strongly suggest you acquire a deck similar to that used in this system, to familiarize yourself with how I see what I see, or as simple a visual deck as you can get. There are a plethora of beautiful Tarot decks available, and later you will find one that suits you personally.

While you're out shopping, select a piece of fabric—special to you, but in a monotone color—in which to keep your Tarot cards (you can also purchase a pleasing box for the same purpose) and on which you will lay them to work them, and a notebook or journal specifically for journaling your daily training.

When you arrive home open the deck and throw away the extraneous cards that always accompany this purchase and, while you're at it, discard the booklet.

Practice Aloud

Find a quiet place and lay out the cloth you have bought, placing the deck on it, face down. Beginning with the one on top, turn over each card and recall as much as you can from your notes by the visuals only, saying as many as you can of the key meanings *out loud*. This is very important, as it establishes the habit of verbal interaction with Tarot. Do this for the entire pack and repeat this a couple more times on the first day.

The Opening Ritual and the 3-Card Read

You will require your journal here to keep a record of your experiments.

In your quiet place, at a self-designated time, open your cards by placing them, one at a time (face down) as in the following diagram. This opens your intention to Tarot—by a time-honored symbol—and will always clear away the energy of the previous client. *Never shuffle them yourself!* Shuffling them at any stage is likely to contaminate the cards with your own future experiences.

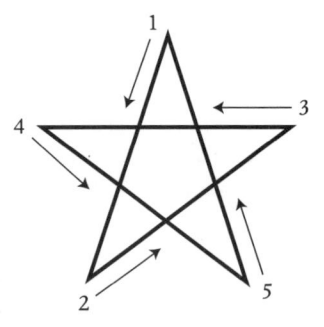

Figure 12: Opening Pentagram

This process is ordered randomness and if none of the cards have stuck together, the last card you lay out will fall on 3.

Pick up the packs in any order and place them together as one pack.

All you are to do, on this night and each of the following nights, is to take the top three cards from the pack and turn them face up, side by side, and recognize what they are saying as a group (exactly like a sentence). You will need all your willpower to refrain from guessing or reading anything to do with you into what you see. Therefore, when you have an understanding of the sentence, say aloud what will happen with the mental intention of recognizing the events the following day in however small or large their capacity.

If you do not do so already, you are to start watching international news on TV, reading newspapers, and/or checking e-news for local and world events because the spreads of three cards may very well reflect these.

Throughout this time it is also advisable to continue refreshing your knowledge of the meanings of each card.

Needing Willing Allies

Wherever possible, this is when you will ask friends if they will allow you to experiment on them and you will use one or more of the layouts in the following study, always opening the cards as described earlier.

Suggest that they also keep a record of what you have foretold and let you know when and if the event(s) occur.

At this stage, please simply keep to basics and do not elaborate or generalize, as these are failings that can become habitual (dooming you to worrying whether you are right or wrong). Only tell what the cards represent.

The more you practice, the more proficient you will become and the greater the chances of flexing psychic muscle.

I suggest you continue training in this vein once or twice a week for several months, slowly introducing more than one spread into your sessions until you have a comfortable half hour or hour's worth of information to give, while constantly refreshing your knowledge of the cards and the application of spreads.

When the phone rings and friends of friends are on the line, telling you that so-and-so recommended you for a session, that is when you will need to establish a method of equal energy exchange—payment of one kind or another. You may wish to begin with a barter system whereby they bring you fresh fruit or vegetables, or other things you might require. When the phone rings often enough you will be in a position to suggest a payment.

UNIT TEN

Tarot Spreads

Section 1: Theory

I am using eight spreads for each consultation. This is excessive for a beginner, but I prefer to give you as much information as possible for you to adapt for yourselves as you progress. These eight spreads are based on four layouts only, as *intention* is what defines the different information.

The four spreads are:

1. *The Celtic Cross*—how one recognizes the information in the initial stages of a consultation.
2. *General Events*—takes you deeper into the events.
3. *Other People and Specific Events ("Every 7th Card" Spread 1)*—significant people or one-time events.
4. *The Tree of Life*—the big picture.

The eight spreads used in a consultation are:

1. *The Celtic Cross.*
2. *General Events.*

3. *Other People and Specific Events.*
4. *The Tree of Life.*
5. *The Warning*—same layout as Other People and Specific Events.
6. *Anything Else*—the same layout as the Celtic Cross.
7. *Destiny (Tree of Life: Ruach)*—Major Arcana Only.
8. *Question*—same layout as for spreads 3 and 5. When you get around to interpreting this spread (you may allow more than one question to your clients) I have given as much advice on the quirkiness of the process as possible without supplying an example spread.

Spread 1—The Celtic Cross (Present, Future, Past)

For this spread, your client will shuffle the cards and cut them into three packs. The client will often ask whether the packs need to be even or whether they should use a certain hand to cut them. My answer to both questions is that it doesn't matter, because it doesn't (unless you decide otherwise).

The pack taken from the top of the deck is always: THE FUTURE.
The pack in the centre of the deck is always: THE PRESENT.
The pack on the bottom of the deck is always: THE PAST.

You will need to watch carefully how the deck is cut because people have many ways of doing so and it is up to you to be vigilant.

Once they have cut the deck you will lay the three packs to the left as in Figure 13, and you will ask the client's STAR SIGN.

If, for example, that person is a Leo, then this person is a Fire Sign and the Queen of Wands becomes the SIGNIFICATOR and will represent the person with you for the entire reading unless you are absolutely certain within yourself that it can also represent someone else.

From this point until Part 2 of the consultation (questions), you are cautioned to advise your client to say nothing to you and to respond as little as possible to what you foresee so that you remain unaffected by them emotionally, and as detached as possible in what you have to tell. Sometimes this becomes impossible because when you hit a sore spot in the client's known circumstances they can easily become quite emotional.

You will need to let your client know that, as the first spread in a sequence of spreads, this layout cracks the cards open and allows Tarot to get to know them; that even though it is GENERAL rather than (in most instances) SPECIFIC, it actually goes to the heart of matters past, present, and future. And it does!

Sometimes these three spreads are so awesome in their information and definition that I wish I didn't have to go further, and I will tell the client so, but they always want to see the rest and so will usually lose the beauty of the moment in the details of the events that ensue.

The cards are then laid out in the following sequence:

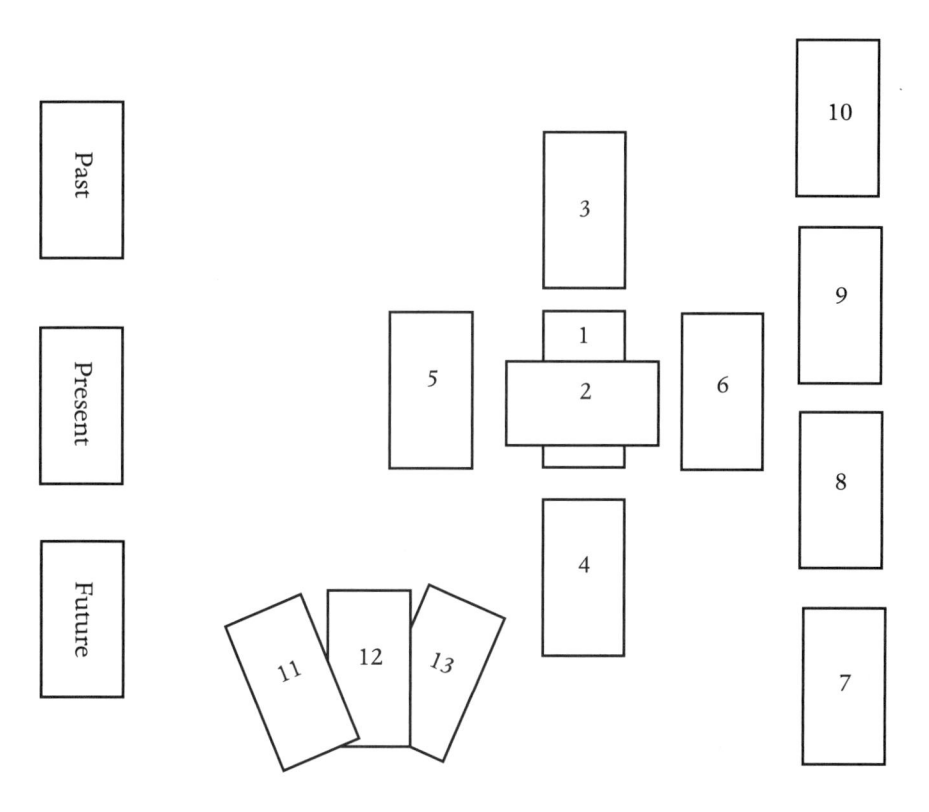

Figure 13: Celtic Cross 1

Once you have laid out the Celtic Cross, you place the remainder of that pack to one side with the card on the bottom of the pack placed on the top, image facing you.

This is called the CROWNING CARD and has deep significance to the overall pattern before you.

You begin with the pack that represents the PRESENT because you want to see what is of immediate influence. You will do the same with the pack representing the FUTURE and, lastly, the pack representing the PAST.

Why I read in this way is because the past is that which remains—for the client—unresolved from their own past, or represents ongoing events of influence, or, in some cases, other people's pasts. The latter is for many reasons: the other person is someone, as yet unmet, who will be important and readily recognized when they begin to talk about themselves; this person is already known to the client and has an ongoing impact in the future, or, sometimes, this other person is body-dead and has left things undone, requiring that the client fix the problem.

The spread on page 177 is a traditional layout with three extra cards fanned to the bottom left. A long time ago I discovered that there was simply insufficient perspective to the original ten-card layout and that by adding the extra information I was able to gain an enhanced, 3D understanding of not only what was right in front of my face, but also peripheral information. You will also discover that I do not quite read them as traditionally as usual because I was not taught from any book or manual.

The following way, however, has always worked for me:

1. The first card laid out is in the centre of your table and this card can (although not always) represent the situation, or person, in the centre of things.
2. The second card is what crosses, adds information, or graces the first card.
3. The third card, laid above, is what is in the person's mind or what is happening at a distance from the situation that has an influence on the spread.
4. The fourth card is the foundation of the spread, what's at the bottom of the situation, or is the environment of the client.
5. The fifth card is a past or current situation that will influence things.
6. The sixth card is what is to follow or where the situation is leading or, if a court card, people likely to influence the situation.

7. The seventh card is the client themselves; who or what represents them or, in the case of a court card that is other than the person in front of you, an ally to your client.
8. The eighth card is the environment—home, work, or otherwise—in which the client will find themselves.
9. The ninth card represents hopes and fears—it has no true reality in terms of actual events.
10. The tenth card is the outcome, or where the events on the table will lead.
11. The eleventh, twelfth, and thirteenth cards are to be read as a whole pattern and will always represent extenuating circumstances or other events that are occurring simultaneously to the above. They can also represent keys for the client's understanding.

Spread 2—General Events

These sets of triplets are all like sentences. They can be read as individual events or they can inter-relate depending on the entirety of the spread. Very often you will encounter correlations to the other spreads. The triplets are read in no particular order but the foundation triplet will always be the strongest influence or the guiding triplet.

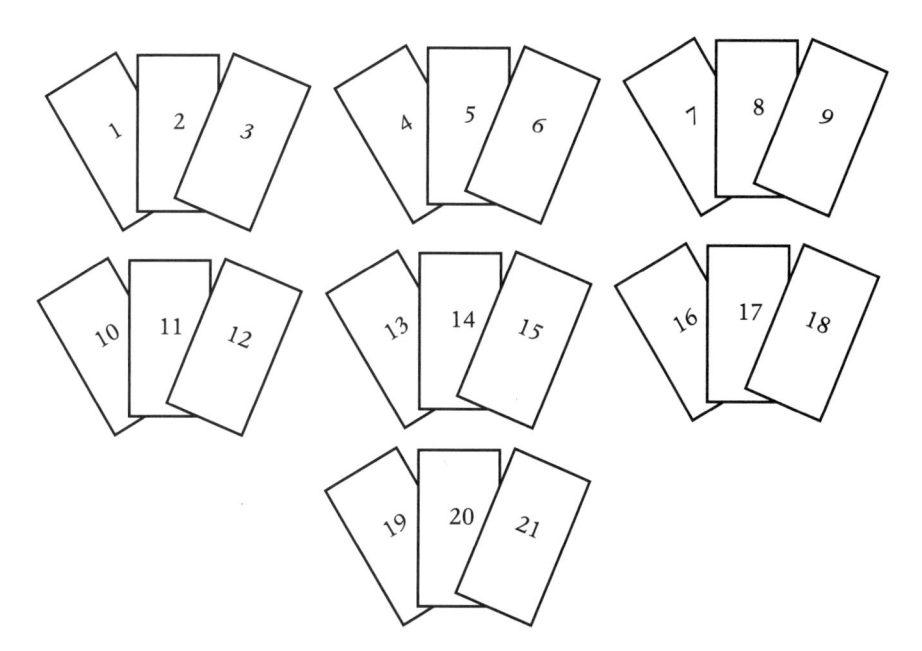

Figure 14: General Events

Spread 3—Other People and Specific Events ("Every 7th Card" Spread 1)

For this spread (and those similar) you will discard the first six cards of the pack and lay out the seventh, face up. Repeat until you have two rows of five cards. Continue the process until the second to last card of the pack, which will be placed at the base of the spread and is considered the foundation of the information.

As the third spread, this is always about people or events that are secondhand to the client but that will have a deep impact through the client's reflection on the event. Things within themselves or their lives are contemplated so that the client can realize certain obstructions or inspirations. Your interpretation will depend on all of the other cards in the spread, and no card will mean anything on its own. This spread will also be read in relationship to anything you have already seen thus far in the consultation.

The layout is the same for Spread 5, the Warning Spread, and Spread 8, the Question (or questions—surmising there are more than one).

Card 11 will always be the signature card or the foundation of events here. The two lines can be one entire event, person, or situation, or each line can be a separate story. On many occasions you will find that the top line is a straightforward situation and the cards from 6 to 10 are underlying influences.

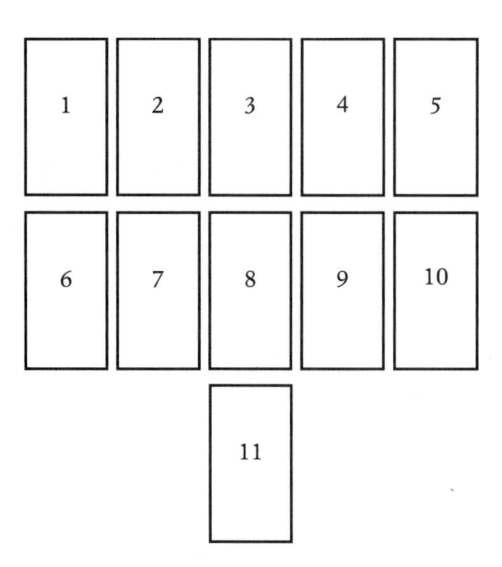

Figure 15: OP and E

Spread 4—Tree of Life

Card 1 represents the four elements and is the foundation of the person's life, where they live; the environment in which they conduct their lives, the state of their lives—all in the future. If you are using this spread for health-related matters, then this position is the feet and legs.

Card 2 represents the Moon and will foretell events that are occurring at a distance or deep thoughts within the client's mind. If using the spread for health matters, this region is the genitals, reproductive and urinary system, or the person's state of mind or any mental condition.

Card 3 represents Mercury and will foretell travel, journeys, and movement of any kind, transportation, communication, and/or the spoken and written word. If using this spread as a health spread it relates to the voice, the vocal cords, the effect of words or communication on either the client or those with whom they have dealings, and, in particular circumstances, the state of one's teeth or any dental considerations.

Card 4 represents Venus and is read in a wide range of ways: it can represent any of the arts; festivals, parties, celebrations; motherhood or a mother or grandmother (the client's or otherwise); sex, intimacy, fecundity, gardening, or gardens. If using this spread for health-related matters, this card will relate to any dysfunctions of the sexuality of the individual, including all sexually transmitted diseases, sexual abuses, or deviant sexual behavior.

Card 5 represents the Sun and so represents the client themselves or those people or situations that have an overpowering or overwhelming influence. The other cards in this and other spreads will inform you as to whether another person falling in this place is an ally or of detriment. In all health matters, card 5 will represent the solar plexus and major organs of the body such as the heart, liver, lungs, stomach, and small and large intestines.

Card 6 represents Mars and this aligns it with everything from family and community to war, unrest and the martial arts. In health-related matters this place represents the gall bladder, the spleen, and the adrenals, and other cards in other areas can aid in identification.

Card 7 represents Jupiter and represents the individual's work and their workplace, their financial situation and their position and reputation in society. In health matters it relates to metabolism, on the one hand, therefore also displaying the person's state of body-mass (or lack of it) in the future, and on the other, any viral, fungal, or bacterial infections, or cancers (anything with the ability to expand).

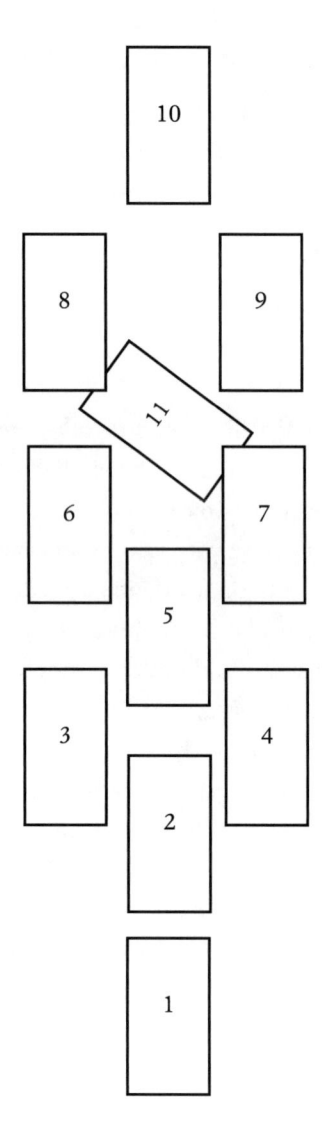

Figure 16: Tree of Life

Card 8 is Saturn's gate. Cards falling here have a relevance to time or duration, to history and all things old or ancient, to institutional bodies of any kind. Health-related issues reflect the skeletal system, the joints, or long-term illness or dysfunction; inherited traits or disease; cultural ideas of what represents health or illness.

Card 9 relates to Uranus and can represent anything from astrology to computer technology, from extreme disorder or chaos to electricity, electrical systems, and nuclear technology. In health matters it refers to the central nervous system.

Card 10 is Neptune and in this position a card refers to the outcome or the next stage of life unfolding, completions, and, in some situations, fame or notoriety. In health matters it refers to the head, one's intellect, the ears, eyes, nose, and mouth (not including the teeth).

Card 11 is called the Key and is represented by Chiron. It gives the client information regarding knowledge not gleaned in orthodox ways; a person of significance who is already known to the client and who will be of assistance at any crucial time; a way of thinking that will be invaluable. In health matters it represents both thought and obscure dysfunctions that defy diagnosis. It is also called the Achilles Heel and is that circumstance which holds one earthbound either physically or mentally, and can therefore represent any culturally stigmatized physical distinction from cross-eyes or a cleft palate to Down Syndrome.

This is a profound overview spread and may have several influences at work:

1. The spread may manifest individual events depending on placement—e.g., card 3, falling in Hod (Mercury) may have nothing in common with events referred to in Geburah (Mars) as indicated by card 6. Card 5 will always represent the significator, events directly relative to the significator or, in the case of Court cards other than that representing the client, either an extreme ally or someone overshadowing the client. You will know this by both the emotion/atmosphere of the spread and preceding recommendations (as very often the people and circumstances repeat themselves for greater clarity).

    Card 10 will represent outcomes or consequences. When Court cards fall here, either the client or other person, there is a sense of either notoriety or achievement. Card 11 is knowledge not gained from academic or traditionally learned sources. In the case of a Court card it is someone already known or who will not remain obscure.

2. Your understanding of the Ruach also means that you will be able to recognize any health or well-being influences in relation to placement—e.g., if the 10 of

Swords falls in 1 there could be foot or leg pain; if it falls in 8 or 9 there is arm or shoulder pain; if it falls in 11 there is likely to be upper back pain; if it falls in 2 it is pain associated with the lower body.

3. The Soul's Journey can also show up here. This will be recognizable by any Major Arcana placement.

Spread 5—Warning

The layout for this spread is the same as for Spread 3.

Spread 6—Anything Else

The client again shuffles the cards and is asked to cut them into three piles. They are asked to choose one pile. You will put the other two piles to one side and only read this pile. The card that is at the base of the pile is the Crowning card and is placed to one side so that its significance is reflected upon during the interpretation of the spread. You will read all the cards, laying out the Celtic Cross as in Spread 1 but *without* cards 11, 12, 13 until all sequences have been interpreted.

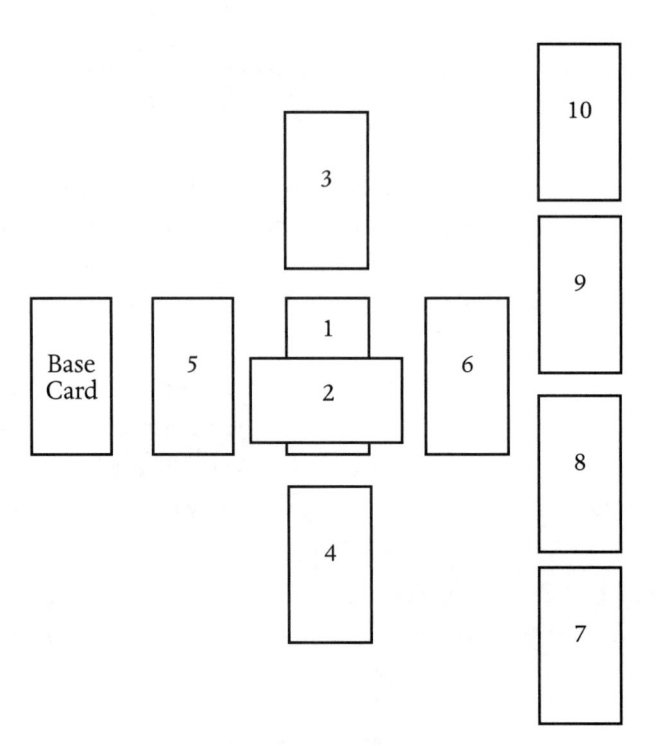

Figure 17: Anything Else

Spread 7—Destiny

This spread is the same layout as Spread 4 but the Major Arcana are separated from the pack and used individually—ideally you will have two packs of cards, one of which is divided into Majors and Minors for the purpose of this exercise.

Spread 8—Question

This spread is also the same layout as for Spreads 3 and 5, but the client will speak their question aloud as they shuffle so that their intention is imbedded into the answering layout.

From now on, until the completion of the consultation, several things are going to happen. First, the gods (whatever you consider them to be), plus the entity that Tarot itself is, will often join in regarding the answers. This can be disconcerting if you are not used to it because if the question is not concise, straightforward, and specific, the answers can vary from hilarious to hostile, depending on the context.

This is where the client will talk with you. You will ask them now to "collapse the wave" by verbally communicating their own concerns, thoughts—anything at all that is important to them *other* than pertaining to what has already been said in Part 1 of the reading—in question form, *while* they shuffle the cards. And here's where glitches can often happen if:

- Their questions are not in alignment with Tarot's understanding of life, love, and the pursuit of whatever.
- The question has no relativity to the future.
- The question flies in the face of the information that Tarot has already given.
- The client asks a generic question such as "Tell me about love," or "Tell me about money," or simply says the word "Relationships."

You will need to ask them what they mean because Tarot requires explicit questions, as one can have a relationship with just about anything. You cannot assume what they mean (Tarot won't), so ask them for clarity as they shuffle.

Tarot will, again, dissuade your client in any way possible if:

- If the answer to their question has already been given in Section 1 then the gods and/or the entity that is Tarot will provide altogether different information, and,

- In the case of naïve questions such as "when will I find my soul mate?" Tarot can be downright rude and obnoxious in its reply.
- If the client seeks to have Tarot remove free will from the equation by asking "should I . . ." or "if I do this or that . . ."

I do warn the client, at the outset, that these variables could occur and if and when they do I always inform them that Tarot is being obnoxious and they have a choice as to whether I give the information. "I'm sorry," I say, attempting compassion, because it is the gods and/or Tarot that has taught me many things about how life really works and so I usually recognize what is going on.

You'll know, believe me, when this is happening because you will understand enough to realize that, as with the soul-mate question, the answer is as likely to be about a cat or dog as it is to be the Devil card or the 7 of Cups.

What do you do if the client is a woman who asks when she will marry and have children and Tarot answers "Never"?

What do you say if the client asks if they will be happy for the rest of their lives and there is the Tower, the 10 of Swords, the Devil card, the 4 of Swords, and the 7 of Cups on the top line; the 8 of Cups, the 5 of Swords, the 9 of Swords, the 2 of Swords, and the Judgement card on the bottom line, with the Death card (meaning "No") as the foundation card? Because it is a stupid question! Life is always full of different events and experiences, of varying degrees of intensity, and so Tarot will seek to educate in its brash and unsubtle way.

Section 2: Two Examples of Full Consultations

Rather than give example spreads without context, I am providing two explicit consultations in a continuum of spreads. If you have the time it is recommended that you record the interpretations of each spread in the sequences and lay out the cards respectively because your first question is likely to be "How does she see that?"

By studying the layout and the recorded interpretation you are looking to understand *holistically* how things work. You will recognize, then, how one spread's information melds with the others. It is like a diagnosis where one has to take several variations of the same or interconnected events into account to give accurate, overall information.

These are two consultations utilizing all eight spreads with both brief example interpretations and in-depth breakdowns of card clusters. Each is based solely on one client at a time to allow you to see the continuum as the consultations progress.

Reminder—NO CARD IS READ IN ISOLATION. No spread is *ever* read as isolated cards, therefore the entire pattern will, in most cases, tell you *one* thing, *one* event or interconnection of events.

Firstly—

- Observe all the cards in the layout, contemplate your sensations and feelings, and understand, in essence (because you have learned all the many various meanings of cards), how they fall together to tell one series of events.
- Until the question time, the consultation should remain unbiased and detached, therefore it is acceptable for your client to remain silent. Quite often you will engender an emotional reaction and a time out for tissues could be necessary.

I will give a brief synopsis on the interpretation before discussing how I have come to these conclusions by breaking down the whole thing into pieces . . . as much as is possible.

Example

Only a couple of days ago I had a client whose question was related to how she sometimes feels at her work. She is an ambulance officer (I've had a few of them) in a local, regional service where this work is still considered "men's work" and she quite often feels that she is put on the spot by the guys.

Her question was "Is there any advice from Tarot as to how I can deal with it better than I do?"

I was horrified, initially, at the answer. My twenty-three-year-old daughter is a gem with a mouth like a razor-blade if she has something to say. She detests what we in Australia colloquially call "whingers and whiners," and has an expression that I find both sexist and rude: "Man-the-f#*%k-up and deal with it!" This is *exactly* what Tarot told my client. I put my hand over my mouth and she asked what it said. I asked if she really wanted to know and she nodded, smiling.

When I told her that I heard my daughter's voice saying what she said, my client roared with laughter. She had expected some deep spiritual advice, you understand. She loved the

1. 5 of Swords
2. 5 of Pentacles
3. 10 of Pentacles
4. Ace of Wands
5. The Chariot
6. 4 of Pentacles
7. The Emperor
8. The Lovers
9. King of Wands
10. The Devil (The Horned One)
11. Queen of Swords
12. 5 of Wands
13. 6 of Wands
Past: 3 of Swords
Present: Queen of Wands
Future: 7 of Pentacles

Figure 18: Celtic Cross 2

answer; said she would use it as her new mantra while at work and that it was perfect for her!

What I will do with a spread like this is to *talk* with my client; to seek to help them to have a juicier and more rounded view of life with all its ups and downs. I will ask that, for example, they go out and purchase a copy of *The Prophet* (my own perennial and much-loved soul mate!) by Kahlil Gibran so that they can read the lines:

> *But if in your fear you would seek only love's peace and love's pleasure,*
> *Then it is better for you that you cover your nakedness and pass out of love's threshing-floor,*
> *Into the seasonless world where you shall laugh, but not all of your laughter, and weep,*
>   *but not all of your tears.*
> *Love gives naught but itself and takes naught but from itself.*
> *Love possesses not nor would it be possessed;*
> *For love is sufficient unto love.*

This section of a Tarot consultation can, by all means, give explicit and amazing answers but it is also a place where the eternal wisdom of Tarot can express itself to its heart's content.

I always allow three questions, and I always use the same spread as for the Warning spread.

As mentioned earlier in this work, when giving some of the meanings of each card, the answer to a person's question is sometimes in the form of a simple *Yes* or *No* and on the odd occasion the answer relates to previously mentioned events that the client might not have heard clearly and, in this case (because you will remember the event or events being queried), the first card on the table will be your answer.

Example 1: Consultation for "Jane Smith"— The Queen of Wands

Spread 1—Celtic Cross

Jane has worked and trained hard to achieve her current place in the world despite how frustrating things may be in the near future (figure 18). There is struggle or aggression based on poverty. She will be in a land or a home divided, and there is much fear. Her words—either spoken or written—will have consequences.

There has been, is, or will be a man with whom there are issues and a woman of importance who is messy by nature but there is no indication as to where she fits into the scheme of things.

Jane will, retrospectively, realize that any hardships, most certainly challenging, have finally passed.

Breaking Things Down

What has influenced the interpretation? What are you looking for on the surface of things in relation to the cards themselves?

First, scan the central theme of the spread and the three cards covering the packs of past, present, and future (as this indicates a generalized progression symbolism).

Note the position of the Chariot card, indicating hard-won victories in the past that influence current circumstances, and let your eye wander in a linear fashion from this card to the 4 of Pentacles.

See what is happening? Can you see the problem?

I have not mentioned the loss or separation (3 of Swords on the pack of the past), because at the moment there is no indication of its significance.

The comment: "*. . . You will be in a land or a home divided and there is much fear. Your words—either spoken or written—will have consequences,*" stems from the composite understanding of Lovers, Devil, and Ace of Wands, the latter card also giving cause for optimism as does the card covering the pack of the future.

The 10 of Pentacles, however, indicates that we are not talking about an owned home here, but rather a rented dwelling or temporary accommodation.

The King of Wands falls in the place of Hopes and Fears so he is an *unsure thing*. It is okay, at this stage, not to pay this card too much attention as he is not in a dominant position. What this indicates is that the client will be unsure of their own feelings regarding this man or one of many other possibilities. I would always wait to see more about him as the reading progresses; he is certain to appear again if he is of influence in the future. If this card was the *Significator* of the client then he is simply worrying. The same applies to the Queen of Swords.

This is a typical spread of a person who has either:

a. Recently completed an educational/institutional program (3 of Swords, Emperor), and who is in the transitional phase of frustration that occurs when they are not yet established in a career that is compatible with their training.

b. Completed a phase of training and has more yet to come (as occurs when an individual is at university) but who has a paper or thesis (Ace of Wands) to write

> c. *Could* indicate an individual working in a poverty-stricken area as the central theme of 5 of Swords/5 of Pentacles indicates. The Ace of Wands indicates she is writing about such things. Should, in subsequent spreads, the work show up distinctly, you will know this is the case.

What is obvious by the 3 of Swords, Lovers card, and 10 of Pentacles is that they are not living in the family home and, with the Devil, both their environment and general situation is threatening.

In reference to the 3 of Swords . . . reserve your judgment until you have read the spread representing the PAST. It will indicate whether it pertains to an environmental change or an emotional issue.

What is also obvious is that this is not a spread indicating ill health, as could happen when Devil and Emperor appear together, and there is also no indication that the institution is of a legal nature.

My final comment
Jane will, retrospectively, realize that any hardships, most certainly challenging, have finally passed, is in direct reference to the 7 of Pentacles—the Crowning card of the pack representing the FUTURE as each of the Crowning cards is a part of each spread.

When you have read all there is to read from the first spread you pick up the cards and hand them to Jane to shuffle again.

Spread 2—General Events

Jane is in a firm, solid position and has her hands in many pies, seemingly capable within all of them. She is deeply involved in both humanitarian and environmental issues.

The entire middle row of cards shows a major environmental disaster, looking suspiciously like a hurricane and given a female name (as so often happens), and Jane will go where the action is in the aftermath of this event. The spread does not indicate in what capacity she acts, although both the earlier spread and the central theme of the layout indicates that there is a crisis over funding or aid and that would not show itself here unless Jane had an involvement in this aspect of things but, in difference to such organizations as *Médecins Sans Frontières*, more in the capacity of aid distribution. That she does this in a smooth, quality fashion, based on honor and heart, is obvious.

The top line indicates that she will spend a great deal of time away from home, but home is secure. There is a big, strong, solid, dependable man in her life who does not appear to participate in her involvement in this event, but there is no indication of children—either there

192   Unit Ten: Tarot Spreads

    1. Ace of Cups   12. The World (Universe)

    2. 3 of Wands   13. 6 of Pentacles

    3. 9 of Cups   14. 9 of Swords

    4. Strength   15. 5 of Swords

    5. King of Pentacles   16. Death

    6. 4 of Pentacles   17. Knight of Swords

    7. Knight of Cups   18. The Moon

    8. 9 of Pentacles   19. Hierophant

    9. Judgement   20. 5 of Wands

    10. Queen of Swords   21. Queen of Pentacles

    11. Tower

Figure 19: General Events 2

are none or they are no longer dependent on family for support, an indication that they are grown and living their own lives.

Breaking Things Down

Please take a look back at the preceding spread (Celtic Cross) and note how things have suddenly opened out.

Let's look at the foundation first: The Hierophant, 5 of Wands, and Queen of Wands (the client). The Hierophant indicates a spiritual, religious, or humanitarian representation and the 5 of Wands is multitasking. I am no longer just looking at this spread in isolation; I am putting two and two together based on the first layout.

The central line of cards in the three groups:

In this instance, the Queen of Swords no longer looks like a person! She is a disaster of massive proportions that has a female name, as do many hurricanes. The fact that in the first spread she was messy by nature is an understatement only from a human perspective. She just does what she does!

The 6 of Pentacles, 9 of Swords, and 5 of Swords indicate aid given to those battling despair, and the Death card, Knight of Swords, and Moon card indicate how quickly this event happens . . . and how deadly it is.

From a personal perspective it has all the appearance of either Hurricane Katrina or the December 2004 tsunami that devastated the Asia-Pacific region.

How do I know it is devastation by water and not some other natural disaster? The Tower is not with the Strength card (which can represent seismic activity), therefore the devastation may have begun with a quake, but it is the Moon card (water) that does the damage (it is not a mudslide disaster either, because the Moon card and the Strength card do not fall together).

Now look at the top line. See how calm it seems compared to the centre?

This reflects, in this instance, the love and backup in Jane's life.

The Knight of Cups, 9 of Pentacles, and Judgement indicates that she brings poise and honesty/quality to the situation, whereas the Ace of Cups, 3 of Wands, and 9 of Cups indicates either a distant achievement and/or love at a distance, and both can be mentioned here as being relevant.

The Strength card, King of Pentacles, 4 of Pentacles? Well, look for yourselves … doesn't the King just exude fortitude and dependability? No matter what his relationship to Jane, he is *not* showing up as any kind of a problem.

194   Unit Ten: Tarot Spreads

                                              1,2,3,4,5

                                              6,7,8,9,10

                         11

    1. King of Cups   7. 6 of Swords
    2. 4 of Cups   8. 2 of Swords
    3. Page of Wands 9. Knight of Pentacles
    4. 10 of Wands   10. The Moon
    5. 2 of Wands   11. The Hierophant
    6. 10 of Swords

Figure 20: OP and E 2

Spread 3—Other People and Specific Events—At a Glance

This one had me perplexed for a moment, but on further contemplation things become clear. The sea is unpredictable and one should never turn one's back on her. She is going to cause some major damage in the future. The Water-sign man (Pisces, Cancer, or Scorpio) or the man associated with water will, therefore, take this into account regarding a project—expect the unexpected. Practical steps will be undertaken to cover all possibilities.

Breaking Things Down

Are we still in the reading for Jane? Yes we are.

So who is this man and why is he significant? Taking into account the previous two spreads, it is easy.

We have a natural disaster by water—hurricane or flood; we have many injured, in need, or simply dead. This spread explicitly discusses a Water sign man or a man associated with the water.

The top line shows the opportunity for major research or a paper to be written. It indicates a coastal environment and also indicates that either he moves there or he is very busy there.

The bottom line indicates that harm from the sea is unseen and therefore work in association with the ocean and/or storm will be undertaken. The 6 of Swords beside the 2 of Swords and the Knight of Pentacles can indicate a submersible craft.

The Hierophant is again present, indicating a spiritual or humanitarian leaning to either/both the man and/or the project.

Again, after reading the last spread, you will take up the cards, neaten the stack, and hand them to Jane to shuffle. You will lay out the Tree of Life Spread. Your interpretation will depend on all cards in this spread and will also relate to anything you have also read thus far in the consultation.

1. The Empress
2. The Magician
3. The Star
4. The Devil (The Horned One)
5. King of Wands
6. 3 of Wands
7. 7 of Swords
8. 2 of Wands
9. Death
10. Knight of Pentacles
11. Page of Pentacles

Figure 21: Tree of Life 2

Spread 4—The Tree of Life

The King of Wands who was mentioned in the first spread now comes into focus.

He is very exploitative to either women and/or the environment. Does he care? No.

He is exceedingly ambitious and will "play the game" to get ahead.

There will be an awful lot of subversion and sneaking around with the aim of expansion and the public will only know part of the truth. I sense a great deal of danger to others or the environment from this man and who or what he represents.

He will travel often and much of his time will be spent in major cities, in five- or six-star accommodations at the behest of either his industry or the government that supports it.

This spread indicates nothing regarding family or friends—this does not mean they are not there, simply that they are the background to the above information.

His motto seems to be "Take Care of Business" and therefore he is governed by economic factors and not humanitarian ones.

I wouldn't be surprised if mining and/or nuclear weapons are his trade or that of an organization he represents. I also do not like the agenda of ego and power that is certainly there although perhaps only suspected by others.

You will know him. How you respond to this knowledge is a matter of free will, personal choice, and safety.

Breaking Things Down

This is a multilayered reading. It allows Jane to understand and, later, recognize the man at the centre of the spread—the King of Wands—when it becomes necessary.

Firstly let your eyes rove over the entire layout and gauge your feelings. Do you not get a sense of dread from the right-hand column; the Pillar of Mercy? Then look at the centre line . . . it is all about the King of Wands, materialism, and power. When your eyes take in the so-called Pillar of Severity all you will notice is a sense of place.

Initially, I recognize that the King of Wands takes up the central position and he has shown up previously only in the position of Hopes and Fears in the Celtic Cross. The very fact that there is so much information on him here (the spread oozes the information that it's all about him) suggests he is highly relevant.

First, he takes the dominant position in the sphere of Tiphareth. This tells me Jane knows exactly who he is; that he is extremely self-aware and that Tiphareth is the sphere of self and should represent Jane but does not! She will know him directly or know *of* him and his dealings. Will he aid or hinder her position in life through his undertakings? He is a political or corporate figurehead and I get a sense that they will not agree.

Look at the sphere of Malkuth (the world; the environment or the place/situation as a foundation). The Empress means many things, but in this position it shows a place of lushness, fecundity, sensuality, and/or luxury. Is the King of Wands here? Is Jane? Chances are the answer relates to both.

Now let your eyes take in the sphere of Netzach (love, sexuality, beauty, art, femininity, fecund environments, etc.). How uncomfortable. What is he doing? Does this represent the plunder of the Earth or is he aware of it and offended by it? Does it represent his sexual biases or his awareness of such? Is Jane affected by the above? Most probably both.

As we travel up this pillar and see the sphere of Chesed (expansion, philosophy, religion, education, etc.) we see the 7 of Swords so all is not obvious and there is a sense of espionage or a hidden agenda behind events. This could relate to Jane's subterfuge in discovering information, or to either the lack of honesty of the King of Wands *or* how he goes about finding out information (either adverse or providential).

In Chokmah (known spiritually as the Sphere of Wisdom but ruling technology, energy, and all things electrical) we see the Death card. What does it tell us? Shudder! Is he involved in a cult such as those seeking a biblical End of Days? Is he involved in nuclear technology of a nature such as WMD? Does he or his dealings close off the door to wisdom and deep understanding? Whatever you decide here, there is nothing comforting about the pattern.

Could it *also* (on the other hand) describe Jane or the King of Wands *preventing*—or being involved with a group that prevents—a threat? Could very well be, but Kether informs me that this would only be a stop-gap measure as it represents ongoing business, financial and/or practical undertakings showing us that the events do not complete themselves here. If the Knight of Pentacles represents Jane then she will continue her course of action.

The Star card falls in the sphere of Hod (long and short journeys, communications) and again many things come to mind: that he is a public—even famous—person; that he flies a great deal; that he is involved with the media in some or many ways; that his agendas have long-into-the-future and/or far-reaching consequences. It could also represent Jane and her long-distance flights/involvement with media. My intuition says all of the above.

The 3 of Wands in the position of Geburah (family, community, warrior, martial or military dealings) points either to Jane, or to the King of Wands, being distant. From what? From family and home? From the ramifications of the actions of the King of Wands? Does it also possibly show a time sequence of three (years, decades) for his agendas? Does it show that Jane is aware of him, but is at a distance? Again I sense all the above to be accurate.

The 2 of Wands in the position of Binah suggests well-established cities—places of institutional significance—nothing more.

The Page of Pentacles in the sphere of Da'ath simply indicates that all knowledge will be of a practical, material nature and, being the Key, events are to be responded to as such rather than in an emotional manner and also that personal study or research will be involved.

At the time of writing this I was curious and looked up the birth charts of several men in the limelight of current history (2006). I'm not for one moment suggesting this is who we are talking about, but I do find it interesting that Saddam Hussein's birthday is 28 April 1937, making him an Aries—a King of Wands—and that he symbolized apparent detriment. On the other side of the coin is Al Gore who is also an Aries, 31 March 1948, whose recent work in regard to global warming, "An Inconvenient Truth," is likely to have a major impact on the general public. There are many others.

Spread 5—Warning

The same layout as: Other People and Specific Events ("Every 7th Card")

1,2,3,4,5

6,7,8,9,10

11

1. 5 of Swords
2. Strength
3. King of Pentacles
4. Ace of Pentacles
5. Justice
6. The Chariot
7. 10 of Cups
8. Queen of Wands
9. 6 of Wands
10. Ace of Wands
11. Temperance

Figure 22: Warning

In a previous spread there was mention of the King of Pentacles, and this time the information relevant to him comes to light.

He is a military man! Not only is he a military man, he also appears to be extremely savvy with the legal system or the justice system.

This is what I call a reverse warning insofar as Jane knows or will know this man. and she is to allow him to mediate with her, or on her behalf. She will come out of any legal process unscathed, happy, and with a great victory.

Breaking Things Down

The top line: 5 of Swords with Strength is a battle of some sort. Put these together with a person and you have a warrior. Add that to the Ace of Pentacles (which can mean money or finances, or represent knowledge) and the Justice card, and you have an extremely proficient individual!

The second line shows Jane's response. She is very happy with results after a difficult time (Chariot, 10 of Cups). No doubt at all that she is a writer (Queen of Wands, 6 of Wands, Ace of Wands).

This spread again reminds us of the Ace of Wands in the Celtic Cross and I am of the opinion, now, that our Jane either authors a book or is a journalist. There may be challenges to what she writes but she will win the day when her work is published.

The foundation card is Temperance, showing the mediation process and the harmonizing effect as a result of the King of Pentacle's intervention.

Spread 6—Anything Else (Celtic Cross)

Again I will ask Jane to shuffle the deck and cut it into three packs. I will then ask her to choose one of the packs, informing her that she cannot make an incorrect choice. Once she has chosen I will lay the other two packs to one side. The pack Jane has chosen is read in the described format until I have interpreted the entire sequence.

This has all the appearances of a long-term view of destiny and it is very satisfactory! There is a sense of achievement in worldly matters that will override anything else that may come from following spreads.

1. 10 of Wands
2. 10 of Cups
3. 5 of Wands
4. Queen of Wands
5. The World (The Universe)
6. Ace of Pentacles
7. Ace of Swords
8. King of Pentacles
9. 3 of Cups
10. The Hermit
11. Knight of Pentacles

Figure 23: Spread 6

Breaking Things Down

Jane, as the foundation, is solid and will be aware of all other things in the spread.

She need only continue what she is already doing (Knight of Pentacles). The King of Pentacles in the previous spread is shown here as being in the same house or situation as Jane. He was mentioned previously as a military man and in this situation—due to the central theme of the World card, 10 of Cups, 10 of Wands, and Ace of Wands he pretty much shares her life. Now this life could be the actual family home (as indicated by the 10 of Cups) or the home/world that they share. That they do/will know each other for a very long time is indicated by both the World card (literal or longevity) and the Hermit card (can represent long times, old age, elders). The Ace of Swords indicates both Jane's authority and her awareness of boundaries. This can harmonize also with the Hermit card, indicating that both people can respond individually to situations.

The 10 of Cups coupled with the 10 of Wands can also be read in an altogether different fashion, particularly being followed by the Ace of Pentacles insofar as it can indicate the building or renovating of a house for sale or profit; it can indicate the home being a place of solidity and security away from the 5 of Wands and, with the 3 of Cups in the position of hopes and fears, a place of reunion where possible.

Spread 7—Destiny (Major Arcana Only)—At a Glance

The overall pattern is one of success through orthodox channels. It is an amazingly uncomplicated destiny, but that does not make it at all shallow. The areas Jane is drawn into are structured, yet strong.

1. The Sun
2. The Priestess
3. Judgement
4. The Empress
5. The Lovers
6. Strength
7. Justice
8. Hierophant
9. The Emperor
10. The Chariot
11. The Fool

Figure 24: Destiny 1

Breaking Things Down

This can be read in two ways:

1. I first look at both Malkuth (Sun card) and Kether (Chariot card) as they are mirrors of each other in an expansive fashion. The Sun card indicates that the world in which Jane is born and lives is a world of success and perhaps even affluence. This does not, as can sometimes happen with such, turn the person to extravagances or debauchery, but, instead, demands that she achieve. This is mirrored in the Chariot card, which is achievement through hard work and self-application, always hinting at continued hard work after successive achievements.

The High Priestess in the sphere of Yesod is an innate, introspective and personal spirituality and that may or may not be reflected in religion. This, then, draws my eye to Binah (its relative) where the Hierophant card shows traditional religions "of the Book" with a long history. Religions of the Book are those such as Judaism, Christianity, Islam, and Hinduism.

The Empress card is graced in the sphere of Netzach. Jane has a very clear idea of herself as a woman and appreciates and enjoys life's luxuries which are, or will be, a definite aspect of her life.

Judgement in Hod shows continual change, both in region and in the field of communications. This aspect of Jane's life is not shadowed by any of the Dark Night of the Soul cards and is, therefore, desired and embraced.

The interesting card is Lovers in Tiphareth, the place of Self. It tells me that Jane is a twin or lives twin lives. Taking the preceding spreads into account I am aware of this duality. Her professional and private life cross over, but they are each as strong as the other.

The Strength card in Geburah gives us the representation of Jane's involvement (a) in the world: the military, armed forces, or similar institution, and (b) as a physically fit woman. With the Justice card in Chesed (Jupiter) Jane is philosophically and practically active in the expansive nature of justice, therefore utilizing her position in Geburah for altruistic purposes rather than violent or mindless ones.

It is funny, in a way, to actually have Jane with me because the Fool card in Da'ath (Chiron) indicates that she has no fixed ideology in respect to the Mysteries and is unaware of knowledge from unrecognized sources. This strongly indicates an instinctive strategist rather than a learned one. I reflect back to Yesod here and understand that through introspection or deep thought Jane *is* in touch with the sacred, but may not view her "Aha!" moments as such.

I have already covered the Hierophant so will move to Chokmah and, again, there are government and/or institutional consequences, but here it is in the area of technology and information technology.

The Chariot in Kether indicates a permanent student: one whose life will not cease to teach. As such, at the time of her body-death, there will be no regrets!

2. The other viewpoint of this spread is more localized. The Sun card indicates that Jane has, or has had, children around her. This is reinforced by the Empress and, further, indicates that the children are connected to a long-term marriage (Hierophant). The Strength card, in relation to this, shows her as stalwart in matters of family and community. All else except the High Priestess card are as above. The High Priestess card, in this instance, means that there are aspects of her life/work that, through necessity, she does not disclose to her family.

Part 2 of the Consultation: Spread 8—Question

Until now Jane has said nothing but now she asks the question:

"Earlier in the reading you mentioned *espionage or a hidden agenda behind events* . . . is it possible to clarify the subject?"

The answer is explicit. There are two related incidents: there is exploitation for profit and, in a short period of time, the country or person concerned is left alone or deserted (moreso the latter with the 3 of Swords)—either as a direct consequence or in relation to the hidden agenda. This has devastating results and the country or person is emotionally bereft. It will be a long time before communication is re-established with relevant bodies.

Breaking Things Down

The Strength card and the 6 of Pentacles together indicate payment for resources rather than work. This could be any resource but I can, in the light of current world events, see many countries in this scenario . . . and it does equate more to a country and its inhabitants than a single individual (remember the situation, in the Tree of Life Spread, was the result of the card in Binah). The 4 of Pentacles causes me to think of two things: first, a controlled time for change and isolation, and second, the hoarding of the profits from the plunder of resources. Look what happens next in the top line: Judgement, Hermit. This is the transition to isolation. There is also a hint in all of this of the Strength card representing a hot, dry land such as the Middle East and the Hermit representing the opposite, such as Europe, Britain, or North America (wherever it gets very cold in winter).

1. Strength
2. 6 of Pentacles
3. 4 of Pentacles
4. Judgement
5. The Hermit
6. The Devil (The Horned One)
7. Death
8. 8 of Cups
9. Ace of Wands
10. 4 of Swords
11. 3 of Swords

Figure 25: Question

The second line is the result! Devil, Death can be taken literally here as the plunge into fear, corruption, suppression, and, yes, death. Together they horrify me as there is nothing dignified in the situation. The following three cards—8 of Cups, Ace of Wands, and 4 of Swords—indicate the disappointment and/or stalemate of dialogue. The 3 of Swords is the separation issue in a nutshell.

Example 2: Consultation with 'John Brown'— The King of Wands (Media)

Spread 1—Celtic Cross

1. The Chariot
2. The Tower
3. Queen of Wands
4. The Star
5. King of Cups
6. 8 of Wands
7. Knight of Cups
8. Queen of Cups
9. Queen of Pentacles
10. Strength
11. 2 of Pentacles
12. Justice
13. Death
Past: 5 of Cups
Present: King of Wands
Future: The Priestess

Figure 26: App 2

At a Glance

John is involved in a legal case. Victory is in sight but for the present the challenge is fraught with discord. He shares his environment with the Queen of Cups, although others figure in his life quite prominently. He has some sadness or disappointment behind him, either a loss or grief over a death, and his future indicates an involvement in the mysterious.

Breaking Things Down

John is a Leo and therefore the Crowning card for the current spread—he is the King of Wands. There is no need to go into how difficult the legal matter is (Chariot/Tower) in relevance to the triplet of 2 of Pentacles, Justice card, Death card, is extremely significant and this triplet also indicates a partnership or the dividing up of money/material goods involving either the justice system or police.

The Star card could, at this stage, mean many things, from the light at the end of a dark time to flight away to an altogether different destination than the rural one (8 of Wands) in which the present scenario is unfolding—even to a hint at astrology (reference: High Priestess card), but I'll reserve my judgment until I see more. The Knight of Cups in the place of Self indicates a time of trust and the Strength card as the outcome (which of course, still is malleable) seems to indicate a solid conclusion to current issues.

In the sphere of place is a Queen of Cups, so this woman shares John's environment, although the relationship is not, as yet, forthcoming as is the role of the King of Cups.

In the background, or affecting his thinking, is another woman (Queen of Wands) but there is no indication as to whether she is distant, in his past (although she could very well be the focus of his grieving—see 5 of Cups), or someone he has yet to meet.

This spread is very obscure and at this stage nothing is utterly clear.

Spread 2—General Events

1. 10 of Pentacles
2. Page of Pentacles
3. King of Wands
4. 3 of Swords
5. 5 of Pentacles
6. The Hermit
7. Queen of Swords
8. The Fool
9. 3 of Wands
10. Knight of Wands
11. 3 of Cups
12. 8 of Cups
13. Queen of Wands
14. 10 of Wands
15. Page of Wands
16. King of Cups
17. Judgement
18. 4 of Cups
19. 10 of Swords
20. 9 of Cups
21. Knight of Cups

Figure 27: App 6

At a Glance

You will leave an environment that can get very cold and there is a falling-out with people whom you once considered close. I don't see a home that you own but rather a rented or leased place from which you conduct private business. Opportunity comes to you by way of an offer from a man already known to you.

There will be a strong female ally who is very involved with a writing project and another, unknown and a fairly lengthy distance or time away, who will also be of importance.

You will do something to please yourself that may actually hurt—such as tattooing, piercing, having chiropractic work, or acupuncture—this will cause you to be very happy.

Breaking Things Down

The triplet of 10 of Pentacles, Page of Pentacles, and John represent John's main place of abode and the 3 of Swords, 5 of Pentacles, and Hermit card represent the severance from the cold place. The Queen of Swords, Fool, and 3 of Wands indicates the unknown woman at a distance and the Knight of Wands, 3 of Cups, and 8 of Cups represents the falling-out with others.

The Foundation triplet is blatant in meaning.

By now I am very interested . . . the King of Cups was represented in the first spread without significant relevance, but in this spread he is making an offer or giving a gift. The Judgement card indicates that something about him has changed—or is it change that he is offering?. Also represented here is the Queen of Wands, 10 of Wands, and Page of Wands—the woman associated with words hinted at in the first spread.

These last two triplets indicate that (a) John is in a different place than where he was in the first spread, and that (b) the King of Cups has joined him.

Spread 3—Other People and Events

1. 3 of Pentacles
2. The Moon
3. Justice
4. The Chariot
5. 9 of Cups
6. Wheel of Fortune
7. 6 of Wands
8. 2 of Wands
9. 4 of Swords
10. The Magician
11. The Star

Figure 28: App 17

At a Glance

Revising the legal matter mentioned in the first spread, this time your success is absolute and you are very happy. You are no longer in the rural area where I first saw you but are now closer to the coast. This is a begin again time for you and also an all clear. You have gained freedom and self-sufficiency of a sort.

Breaking Things Down

Top line: 3 of Pentacles is a professional discussion—this (Moon Card) is either covert or outside of a courtroom and, coupled with the Justice card, Chariot, and 9 of Cups, it indicates that an out-of-court settlement is very propitious and satisfactory.

The second line sees the back-and-forth—or return journey—to the city (Wheel, 2 of Wands) as easy, and John is in his element (6 of Wands) and completely comfortable with this. After a small time of relaxation (4 of Swords) John is set to begin his new life in complete independence and self-determination.

The Star card, again, features prominently and reflects a clear future.

Spread 4—Tree of Life

1. The Star
2. Knight of Wands
3. 7 of Swords
4. The Priestess
5. 3 of Swords
6. Hierophant
7. 2 of Swords
8. The Sun
9. 5 of Swords
10. 8 of Pentacles
11. 8 of Wands

Figure 29: App 13

At a Glance

John has had a successful separation from a past partner (either business or marital) and has learned a great deal regarding strategy. His work will be prominent in the future even though it is behind the scenes.

Breaking Things Down

I am now of the absolute opinion that John is in the media or entertainment industry as the Star card is featured here as his way of life/living environment. He is very obviously sitting on a project (High Priestess card) involving sex, sexuality, or women's matters and (7 of Swords) is being very careful with whom he discusses this.

Both the 3 of Swords and the 2 of Swords show him working apart from the hub of the industry but the 4 of Wands indicates he knows it well and knows which festival or gathering to attend.

The Hierophant card indicates ongoing conflict with the past partner and the Sun card can represent two things: long-term, ongoing relationships with his children and success within the established industry.

The 5 of Swords in Chokmah does not bother me . . . he simply struggles with new and, perhaps, future technologies because the 8 of Pentacles, his work, is both acknowledged and gains him recognition.

Getting out of the partnership has liberated him and working as he is in a freelance style is perfect for both his career and his self-worth.

Spread 5—Warning

1. Ace of Wands
2. Queen of Swords
3. Ace of Swords
4. Knight of Pentacles
5. 2 of Pentacles
6. Justice
7. Hierophant
8. Page of Cups
9. 8 of Cups
10. Page of Wands
11. King of Wands

Figure 30: App 18

At a Glance

There is nothing in the spread that relates to either love or the lack of it but, in consideration of all I have read so far, the understanding is inherent in the information. John has a future opportunity to work on a partnership project with a woman who appears to be a writer/editor. There is nothing to indicate that he should not do so but he has been bitten by a legally binding marriage in the past so must consider how any legality is handled . . . read the fine print, John!!

Breaking Things Down

John (King of Wands) is the foundation of this spread so must consider himself first in the upcoming situation. He will encounter a woman (Queen of Swords) who is a writer/editor (Ace of Wands to her left, Ace of Swords to her right) who comes forward with the financial proposition (Knight of Pentacles) of a partnership (2 of Pentacles).

The second line first gives us the Justice and Hierophant cards together, which is that legally binding marriage (not love), but it is followed by a Page of Cups and 8 of Cups. These indicate that if John is not emotionally mature in response to the situation he will be belittled or reduced (Page of Wands as John made smaller).

Spread 6—Anything Else (Celtic Cross)

1. The Empress
2. The Magician
3. 5 of Cups
4. Queen of Pentacles
5. 4 of Swords
6. 9 of Penacles
7. 9 of Swords
8. 5 of Pentacles
9. 5 of Swords
10. 10 of Swords
11. Knight of Pentacles

Figure 31: App 4

At a Glance

A woman is hurt, ill, or betrayed. This spread indicates that the woman is used to being very powerful and independent.

Breaking Things Down

Because this is anything else, the subject of this spread (Queen of Pentacles) has not been mentioned at all so far. Whoever she is and whatever the relationship is between her and John is not mentioned either, and yet his response is shown (Knight of Pentacles).

The Empress and Magician together show her power and influence, even her knowledge of herself, and the 9 of Wands shows her used to being mistress of her own life, yet the lead-up to the events is 4 of Swords, so either she did nothing to cause the following events or she was lazy in dealing with whatever needed to be done to perhaps stave off the events.

Every other card shows her devastation! In the sphere of Self she is ill, worried, unable to sleep, or heartbroken (9 of Swords); in the sphere of the environment in which she lives there is nothing, poverty, loss; in the sphere of hopes and fears there is conflict, either personal or with others (and I doubt very much that this is a hope!); in the sphere of outcomes is the pain, brutality, or betrayal; and in the sphere of mind or distance there is mourning or grief.

What will John do? That is for another time and the only indication of his direction is his practicality.

Spread 7—Destiny

1. Hierophant
2. Wheel of Fortune
3. The Emperor
4. The Moon
5. The Priestess
6. The Lovers
7. The Fool
8. The Hermit
9. The Hanged Man
10. Strength
11. The Magician

Figure 32: Destiny 2

John's life destiny in the world (Malkuth) is the Hierophant and in this case it represents marriage, both to the world at large and individually (marriages are all contractual or defined, whether loving or business) and the current and future events in the preceding spreads attest to this. I look from Malkuth to Da'ath (knowledge) and understand that his self-knowledge and ability to work independently within these unions is all-important.

The Wheel of Fortune in Yesod (and the lack of the Judgement card) informs us that this will be so for the entirety of John's life.

On the right-hand pillar: the Moon card in Netzach is both graced and detrimental: in its graced state it shows that John will have much to do with images; that his destiny will "water the garden." In detriment it shows that intimate relationships will cause him disillusionment, whereas, above this in Chesed we see the Fool: he does not necessarily seek the public eye but will have it thrust upon him anyway.

The Hanged Man in Chokmah, which on the one hand represents Wisdom and on the other, in a more worldly sense, technology in all formats: he gains detachment and altruism as he ages. He will be aware of his destiny and at some stage in his life he will come to realize that life really isn't about choices so much as surrendering to fate as it unfolds.

The left-hand pillar: the Emperor in Hod tells us that he will be well-educated and will deal with corporations or establishment bodies and will be known as an authority in communications, whereas, just above this in Geburah, is the Lovers card. This informs us that where family and community is concerned he will be divided—both a part of and apart from. John needs to realize that his public life will not give him the opportunity to simply settle and be a normal father or partner; he will be away sufficiently enough to have this cause distress unless he is wise.

Above this, in Binah, is the Hermit. This is simple: John will not die young.

Back at the central pillar, the centre of the Tree, is John himself: the High Priestess Card. This card falling in this position causes all tension to drop from our shoulders because he *will* be wise and he *will* see life from the perspective of wonder and mystery; he will also have a deeply private aspect to his nature. People might think they know John but no one will truly know the depths of the man, as this card indicates that he sees things that others may not; understands things that others cannot.

The Strength card in Kether (the mirror of Malkuth) indicates a deep fortitude of mind and also the constitution of an ox. When he finally experiences body-death he will leave it with ease and not frailty. This final indicator will be potent for John as it symbolizes, as an example, an old man who simply dies in his sleep without extended illness or loss of mental/physical faculties.

Spread 8—Question

1. Page of Wands
2. King of Wands
3. 7 of Wands
4. 3 of Wands
5. King of Swords
6. 6 of Swords
7. 5 of Swords
8. Queen of Pentacles
9. 10 of Pentacles
10. The Lovers
11. Judgement

Figure 33: App 19

John makes the observation: "There was mention of pain, I think, earlier … and yes, I've got "mouse" shoulder—RSI I think—from too much time at the computer. I am inspired by the last spread but would still like reassurance regarding any other health issues in the near future."

At a Glance

Not of the physical kind—just a stressful living arrangement that will need to be resolved.

Breaking Things Down

John will make contact with a colleague of a friend (King of Swords) at a distance. Due to the presence of the Page of Wands, there is indication that John has known the other man for many years. I have no doubt that this man turns up. The question here is (a) whether John is, at the time, already sharing his space with the Queen of Pentacles (who makes life difficult as a result of the friend being there) or (b) whether he brings her with him. One way or another there will be some conflict and struggle regarding shared accommodation or housemates (6 of Swords, 5 of Swords, Queen of Pentacles). The Lovers card indicates that (a) John will need to choose between the two, or (b) there will be sexual tension that will require resolution.

Part Four
The Future

UNIT ELEVEN

Understanding the Way

There is no Tarot without Magic.

Theory: Tarot Itself as Teacher—Personal Detachment

There are only so many things that can be learned from a book—one of the basic reasons I have refrained from writing this for so many years—because Tarot (the power beyond the cards) is that which ultimately teaches you to recognize new meanings. Being open to this force is what all the prior theory has been about, because experience has taught many people that uneducated dabbling with Tarot backfires.

I've known of people who will get together and attempt to read Tarot over and over, seeking to see what they *want* to see and dealing out spread after spread until they think they have an outcome that suits them. The trouble is that everything else they have dealt out is going to also happen, so that if a series of disasters or unfortunate events is predicted on the way to seeking something ultimately pleasant, then, in the nature of Unit 1—*The Chicken or the Egg*—the interpretations of discord will not go away and ultimately must occur.

The same applies to thinking that Court cards (people cards) might be someone you know, because this is all assumption—when people fool around like that they have no objectivity, and the whole thing becomes almost (if not absolutely) dangerous.

This is the case in assuming that cards always mean what you originally learned they meant, because that will change as current history changes.

When I began learning Tarot (back in the late 1960s) the world was a far different place and such things as AIDS, in vitro fertilization (IVF), same-sex marriage, nuclear proliferation, uranium-depletion, nanotechnology, the commonality of tattooing, and the internet were utterly incomprehensible. When, eventually, these things became considerations I had to recognize them. Therefore the more the reader can keep up with current events, the better equipped they will be for accurate foretelling, because Tarot knows and will tell you, and, believe me, this can be disconcerting.

Once you gain a reputation as an accurate reader, people will come from everywhere and from all backgrounds and one can never tell, from appearances, who those people are or the way of life they lead. You must trust Tarot and say what you see, despite what you think.

Bear in mind that it is important for the reader to be unswayed by the client so that they are to tell you nothing about themselves or their lives during the first phase of the reading (foretelling) up to where they discuss with you, during phase two—question time—whatever it is that they want to know. This may very well have been answered one way or another during the first phase, but due to the usually relentless barrage of information given during this phase the client is unlikely to have registered all that you have said and will only do so in retrospect when they listen back to whatever device you have used to record the reading.

The names given in the following case histories are fictitious.

Case History—Jane

Jane was in her early fifties, had short, blonde, well-cut hair, and was dressed in casual summer clothing and minimal jewelry. She looked "city" (in contrast to the local people here in Byron Bay) and had an American accent. Had I been asked, based on appearances, to guess either her lifestyle or profession I would have been hard-pressed to do so. I would have presumed she was not financially secure, but that she lived a so-called ordinary life, whether that was here or in the USA.

That's not what Tarot told me. I saw death and destruction, governmental institutions, clandestine activity, lots of international travel, war and violence, and paradox after paradox, because she was obviously married and successful, and had a beautiful home and grandchildren.

1. The Tower
2. 10 of Cups
3. 5 of Swords
4. The Emperor
5. 7 of Swords
6. Queen of Pentacles
7. 2 of Swords
8. 8 of Pentacles
9. 6 of Wands
10. Ace of Swords
11. Hierophant

Figure 34: Tarot Itself as Teacher 1 Bosnia

This is an example of what might have turned up on the table concerning this woman. Please really contemplate the images, even without going into later card-interpretation-breakdowns, because it is your ability to see—by way of the above Tree of Life, discussions, and associations—what I see.

Breakdown

The first thing I am going to do is take an overall look at the pattern, then I'm going to take a deep breath and launch into what, from my perspective, is a very difficult and "heavy" interpretation. Please take into account that a reading will have many spreads to its advantage and therefore the bigger picture and other events will be brought to bear in your interpretations.

The Blasted Tower in the position of Malkuth shows me the world in which the client will live or be. It is one of major upheaval and disaster. The Tower in this position can represent explosions or extreme violence, chaos, and disorder, along with the toppling of people or positions of authority, whereas in Yesod you can see the *10 of Cups*, indicating that her true home is elsewhere (as this is one of Yesod's meanings).

When you do a spread like this it isn't progressive—it doesn't necessarily follow any order like the Lightning Flash, although it can—and you need to look at both the big picture and each sphere individually.

When I see the Blasted Tower, particularly in this position, I am going to look for the causes elsewhere because it could as easily be a house-fire, a bomb, or a natural disaster. What it always will be, however, is the person and/or the person's world and, again, the other cards will tell you which.

I see the *Emperor* in the sphere of Netzach, an unusual place for this card to fall, and the *8 of Pentacles* (work) in the sphere of Binah (representing government, administration, tradition, or institution). Therefore I am certain that this woman will be involved in a government job and will also be other than a simple employee *because* of the Emperor card, which places her in a position of power, as a woman in a typically man's world.

Where's the clue? Of course! My client is the *Queen of Pentacles,* which falls in the sphere of Geburah which is associated with Mars. Dare I say she's a warrior? Dare I say she is in the military in a war-torn environment? That's *exactly* what I'm going to say.

It takes me a while to work out the *7 of Swords*. It falls on Tiphareth, which represents the Self, so what's she doing sneaking around like that? And why is the *2 of Swords* (one of its meanings being silence) in Chesed, which can represent the person's workplace among other things? Hmm.

With the *Ace of Swords* at the position of Kether I can say nothing more than to reiterate that she will be in a position of power in a military institution with silence and secrecy surrounding her life.

The *Hierophant* in the position of Da'ath could have meant many things, but I simply opted to say that her marriage was her key to success, because in earlier spreads I'd noted how happy this part of her life was.

She told me about herself during question time. She is a colonel in U.S. Military Intelligence, and was on holiday from her work. She was, at the time of her reading, stationed in Bosnia during the international armed conflict that took place in that region from 1992 to 1995 and, even though many events that were predicted were yet to be comprehended, the majority of what I had told her was already known.

Case History—Robert

Robert has been a client of mine on and off for about twenty years, coming once every two or three years for his next reading. He is a very successful man in his early thirties who lives in both Australia and the USA.

1. The Star
2. The Tower
3. Death
4. 10 of Swords
5. The World (The Universe)

Figure 35: Tarot Itself as Teacher 2, 9/11

This was the top line of one of his spreads in June, 2001:

Not only did this spread show up for Robert, but over the coming days and weeks the first three cards turned up many times in the exact same sequence.

This spread cannot be taken to pieces. It reads as a pictorial story and that story tells of something from the sky exploding and, because the *Death* card and the *10 of Swords* together represent violent death, the outcome to the first two cards is obvious. The final card in the line, *The World*, says one of two things: (a) that the outcome to this event is a worldwide event, or (b) that the event heralds a new cycle.

Either way, the prophecy is the same, and Robert was in New York when the World Trade Center exploded.

What is interesting in retrospect is that in the days following September 11, I was with friends at a local café, talking about the event and talking about the Tarot reading, which I had conjectured over with them when I had first recognized the crisis. The chef, an acquaintance for whom I had read several years before, and who was also sitting with us on his break, informed us that the prediction of towers blowing apart, etc. had been in his reading *three years prior!* The mind boggles, even after all these years, at how Tarot can tell these things.

Case History—Jenny

Jenny was in her early twenties, very overweight, very plain. She wore simple silver jewelry.

As I progressed through her reading, it became obvious that she was happily married. Tarot kept on and on, spread after spread, about the birth of a child, but accompanying this information were very peculiar cards. There was disappointment on more than one occasion, and sadness and grief. There was also a sequence of patterns that initially made no sense to me (I don't recall the *exact* layout but the following is close enough).

The first thing that caught my attention was the obvious birth of the *Page of Cups* because the *Ace of Wands* and the *Sun* card together means "birth," almost always of a biological infant, no matter the species, although, as an animal other than human, the *Strength* card is sometimes depicted.

What confused me initially was the top line and what it had to do with the outcome. Yes, it is the number of times my client is to be, or has been, disappointed by IVF treatments.

1. The Empress
2. Ace of Swords
3. The Emperor
4. 4 of Swords
5. 8 of Cups
6. Wheel of Fortune
7. Page of Cups
8. Ace of Wands
9. The Sun
10. 4 of Wands

Figure 36: Tarot Itself as Teacher 3 birth

Once I got it, her eyebrows shot up and she could not help but inform me that she and her husband had been married for five years (she was older than she appeared) and that they had had three attempts to date at in vitro fertilization, all of which had failed.

I informed her to not change what she was doing because they were most assuredly going to have a baby, but from my perspective, because of the *Wheel of Fortune*, it would occur naturally.

I ran into her in Woolworth's a few years later. She was still overweight, but she had a baby in her arms and was glowing. She told me that she and her husband had paid for four more attempts and all had failed. They had given up.

She had thought nothing of it when her menstrual cycle hadn't come because it had always been irregular and she only went to see her doctor when she found herself constantly nauseous. The child had been conceived, and was delivered at home by a midwife and Jenny's husband.

Always remain detached from including your own opinions or advice and always remain open to the unexpected and that which appears utterly unbelievable, as it is not the reader as an individual that is important but as a *vessel* through which Tarot can inform what it knows.

Divining for Yourself or Those Close to You

Simply put, this can backfire. If you or those close to you (friends and family) want to seek out a psychic it can be preferable to ask around for someone with a reputation for accuracy and suggest they see them instead. The same applies to anyone whose life you know too well, as you may have difficulty with objectivity and be prone to assumptions.

A good example is last Monday: my daughter and her friend flew to Melbourne. The friend's mother drove the girls to the airport and dropped by my house on her way back. We had coffee and chatted for an hour, getting to know one another. Toward the end of the conversation she asked if I would read Tarot for her and I informed her it was too late; I already knew too much about her. If she had asked beforehand I would have forestalled any conversation and simply made the booking.

In circumstances whereby I know people well, but they have been away for an extended period of time, I am able to read for them as long as they do not inform me of what they have been doing. It is as though the mystery of people's lives allows for clarity.

The Fear Factor: Telling Bad News

Why do I do it? Why do I read for others and put myself through the often harrowing experience of telling people what I see, despite what the news can sometimes engender?

There are many reasons, but ultimately it is the gift of grief relief, and some examples, again, are necessary:

Case History—Fred

This reading occurred during a time when I lived in rural Victoria. A man in his sixties—I'll call him Fred—was talked into coming to see me by his wife and adult daughters. I felt that he really didn't believe in what I was doing but had come simply to please them. When I sense this (and it can be quite common), I offer a choice and tell the person that it's okay to just leave and that it's better that they do so if they are not there of their own free will. Fred said, "No I'll stay."

I vividly remember telling him that, in the cards representing the past, I saw him weeping for a man he had never met and that he had the marks to remind him of it always, and that it had changed his life.

Fred was visibly shaken and asked if I would stop the reading, which I did. He reached over and lifted a trouser-leg to just below the knee. He had a savage scar that wrapped almost all the way around his calf. He proceeded to inform me that he'd been driving home from the pub one night with too much alcohol in his system. He had veered over the double lines and had hit a motorcycle head-on and the bike had spun out of control, ending up off the road. Fred's car had slammed into an embankment and his leg had been cut wide open as the driver-side door had imploded with the impact.

Fred had forced his way out of his car and gone over to the victim—a young cop in his early twenties who was critically injured.

There was no mobile phone, it was the middle of the night on a dark country road and Fred had sat, removed the young man's helmet, and had held him in his arms as he died. He had stayed there like that until finally another vehicle had shown up. Its inhabitants had assessed the situation and the woman had stayed with Fred, who by that time had lost a lot of blood from his own injury, while the driver went off to phone for help.

Fred has never gotten over the event. He had been charged with negligent manslaughter and had spent time in prison, had never drunk a drop since and had never stopped feeling guilty. He didn't want me to read anymore, he just stayed and talked to me for a while longer, telling me he was thankful for someone to talk to about the incident, as his family had never wanted to discuss it.

Case History

The second example was a woman (I'll call her Anne) for whom I could see intense anguish over the death of a loved one for whom she had never mourned.

Anne was a psychiatrist who had been deeply in love with a fellow practitioner and had an affair with him that had lasted several years. He was married and had children and had not wanted to leave his family. Anne, being very sophisticated (she thought), had agreed that it didn't matter.

She had remained silent about the affair, afraid that someone would say something to let the cat out of the bag and so, when her lover died of cancer, she had kept up the ruse and had never mourned until someone (me) had told her what she already knew. She wept. The last thing she said before she left after the reading was that life was uncanny in a way—she was a psychiatrist who, in those days, charged eighty dollars for a visit, and said nothing, whereby someone like me only charged (in those days) twenty-five dollars and did all the talking. She called me "the poor man's psychiatrist."

Case History

The thing about keeping records of readings by way of cassette tape or other recording device is the retrospective impact. Ron was another client. He had been to me on more than one occasion, but this day I saw the death of a relative by their own hand and that no one was to blame and that it would be this relative's destiny to do this thing.

Ron came up to me in the street of my hometown a year or so later and told me what had happened. His mother's sister and her family lived on the other side of Australia. His cousin had committed suicide at age twenty-eight by hanging himself. The family was devastated because he had left no note and had shown no signs of being unhappy. Each of them was wracked with guilt.

When they had contacted Ron's family, he had flown over, taking the tape with him. He played it to them, and even though they were still really sad, the affect of having an unknown psychic describe the event beforehand was, in a way, like Ron's cousin having left a message and relieved them, partially, of the pain of wondering why he had done such a thing, and whether any of them could have prevented it from happening.

Case History

There was Sally, whose reading looked for all the world like that of someone getting ready to die and who was busy putting her affairs in order. I told her over and over that her kids and her husband would be okay; to relax and be at peace because they would be able to cope. At the conclusion of the reading she informed me that she had asbestos-related cancer and that having a stranger tell her about the outcome for her family was the most important thing for her and she could die without worrying for them.

Case History

There was June—a woman in her fifties—whose cards were so packed with domestic brutality against her that I wept. She sat stunned as, in spread after spread, I lost my cool and suffered her emotions throughout (I'll get onto that soon). At the conclusion of the reading she talked about being in this very bad marriage for over thirty years and attempting to protect her children from the effect of this man's actions on their well-being. I told her that they knew; that they had always known. She asked me what she should do and I told her it was not my job to tell her that, that how she responded to what I saw was all about free will. I held her for a long time while she cried.

Her own mother was sitting in my garden, waiting for her turn, and after the reading I went outside and said that I was sorry, after what I'd experienced of her daughter's life I was too upset to do another reading.

One of my students of Tarot was June's sister, and June, her mother, and her sister went afterward to a café where June told them exactly what had been going on all these years. Both mother and sister were shocked.

June came back to me after three years, a changed woman. Once the demon was out of the bottle she'd spoken to her son and daughter, who said, "Yes Mom, we always knew." They backed her up when she left her husband, and through all the court proceedings. Eventually, when the magistrate had heard everything, he asked the husband why he had done those things to his wife and the husband had answered that she had deserved every beating. The magistrate decreed that the husband got nothing from the marriage. June got everything. She has since traveled and moved house and put her life back on track.

There are too many examples, but you get the idea. Tarot will sometimes help people to get the best price on the sale of a property; it can warn people about deceptions in business dealings and about dangers yet to come, but it cannot prevent events occurring, and it will not take away free choice. A cool example is that of a man who approached me regarding his investments on the stock exchange. He offered me huge sums of money if I could tell him the best deals.

Unfortunately, I told him, if Tarot says you will lose money, then no matter where you put it you will lose it. I recall a client back in 1987. I was upset by this man's reading, saying, "You poor bastard, you've got nothing!" He'd been most displeased by my interpretation and grudgingly paid me for my time, sneering at me because he had three-quarters of a million dollars invested in the stock exchange. He returned three weeks later to apologize. That was the time of the October 1987 crash and he'd lost almost everything.

The Spoken Word: The Literal Truth

The actual way you tell of the events is also very much an aspect of the readings, and Tarot is peculiar in this. I will cite three examples, but before that I will discuss the question/answer section of a session. This takes place (should you choose to use it) at the second phase of the consultation, after you have prophesied the events you have seen without the client's input. At this phase they are told they can have Tarot answer a specified number of questions. They are asked to talk the question through with you and by doing so they are collapsing the wave (refer to Unit One—The Chicken or the Egg). You will need to explain that even though it can be nonspecific in nature, the question cannot be too broad in its wording. Any question such as "Tell me about relationships" will need to be clarified with the client. *I know* what they mean, but it's not me who provides the answer, it is Tarot. If the person does not specify, then Tarot could talk about family, or the car, or their workmates, or their dog! It does it out of a sense of humor (because Tarot definitely has one).

Questions about offspring will always be answered, as Tarot seems to love children and cares about their welfare, but really stupid questions, or questions that have been blatantly answered in the first part of the reading will be treated with disdain.

So on to the examples of literality.

Case Histories

Bob was someone I'd known for quite a while, but had not seen for several years. Somewhat of an anti-establishment-everything kind of guy, he was adamant I was wrong when I told him that I saw him marrying someone. Within a year he had auditioned for a production of Shakespeare's *Romeo and Juliet* and had won the part of the friar who married Romeo to his Juliet.

His long-time friend Jill had also come for a reading on the same day. In her future I'd seen her married to a Scorpio man and that they had a seventeen-year-old daughter. That prediction ended up being quite a debacle because she also auditioned for the same play and won the role of Lady Capulet. Her stage partner, Lord Capulet, was played by a Scorpio man whom Jill fell for head over heels in real life, thinking to herself that the very handsome man was to be her husband in the future, that they would have a daughter together, and would still be together when the child was seventeen years old. Assumptions are dangerous things. The Scorpio man was gay and Jill set about attempting to convince him that he really wasn't. It was apparently very tragic and very funny, depending on the perspective. The realization struck her regarding the true nature of the reading when the girl who was cast to play Juliet turned out to be seventeen years old!

Tarot said that it looked like Amelia (a local woman whom I knew as an acquaintance) was coming into money, and that it would be a gift that had to do with someone living in England. Amelia was very excited because she had a wealthy uncle living in London.

She phoned me some months later to tell me that her uncle had made contact and that for tax purposes he actually had to give away some money. She told me he was sending her

8,000 pounds, and she intended to set up shop in town, a thing she had wanted to do for years. I quite flippantly said to be careful because the money wasn't in the bank yet, but she laughed, refusing to have her good mood dampened.

I saw her in town a couple of weeks later and she wanted to show me the shop that she was due to sign the lease on. We had a look. She said that the money was to be transferred into her bank the following day. I asked her exactly what Tarot had said and she knew; she had it learned by heart: "It explicitly said, 'It looks like you're coming into some money.'"

I replied, "Well, it doesn't actually say that you *are* coming into money." But again she refused to be put off. The following day she phoned me, most upset. It had been *a* thousand pounds, not eight; she had misheard what her uncle had said. All her plans were cancelled.

I saw Mary getting on a plane for an all-expense-paid trip to Japan that she would win through a competition. Mary laughingly told me when she came for another reading that it had been her identical twin (who lived in another state) who won the trip!

The Plateau

It is inevitable, once you have studied and begun reading for others, that you will hit a plateau, whereby you have no feedback from clients, they seem confused when you are reading for them, or you feel that you are getting nothing psychically but are merely interpreting by rote. This happens for everyone and can be very disconcerting. It is the *make or break* phase when Tarot tests the individual to ascertain whether they have both the fortitude and the self-trust to continue. The process may last several weeks, even months, and if you falter here you will not become a vessel through which Tarot communicates. In all the years of teaching I have only ever known four students to successfully pass this phase and only two of them went on to become professional readers with solid reputations for accuracy.

When the phase is over you will know it. You will encounter a breakthrough reading whereby the client will confirm, even at the table, the accuracy of what they *already* recognize as pertinent to their lives. From then on you may have small periods of plateau but never to the same degree.

Myth and Legend: The Morality of Tarot

One significant way to understand Tarot is to understand myth and legend. What myth and legend are *not* are fabrications or illusions. All myth and legend stem from historic events that transform over time to become the symbolic or allegorical[1] representations of that history or the respective culture.

What is significant is that myth and legend applies to every individual that you will ever encounter, including yourself. To know this is to have wisdom on your side when you work with others. Otherwise it is very easy to become lost in the seeming day-to-day that is never still, only sometimes lying in a state of waiting.

There are always special children (or quests); there is always murder and mayhem, usurpation, betrayal, intrigue, valor, hopelessness. There is always a savage, otherworldly place of trial and tribulation where searching, yearning, being lost, and going to the brink of madness (and sometimes falling in) takes place. There is always redemption and there is always succession and death.

In the world of the individual these events can take place over a lifetime or a week. In the world of nations, cultures, friendships, and communities it is the same.

What are we to make of this in our own lives? That fate allows for no mistakes, only experiences. This is a powerful understanding that removes us from the board of the blame-game, and a broader vision and perspective become achievable.

People, communities, and nations alike are all the product of standards of morality and concepts of right and wrong that Tarot doesn't necessarily adhere to. To be quite honest, it does not judge, but tells, and therefore the more adaptable the reader—the more worldly-wise—the greater the ability for accurate prediction.

---

1 Allegory is a figurative mode of representation conveying a meaning other than, and in addition to, the literal. Through allegory a subject of a higher spiritual order is described in terms of that of a lower, which is made out to resemble it in properties and circumstances, the principal subject being so kept out of view that we are left to construe the drift of it from the resemblance of the secondary to the primary subject.

UNIT TWELVE

Going Professional

Walking the Walk

It is suggested that you begin your career in a simple manner by making yourself available at markets or fairs, charging only small sums of money to begin with and doing only fifteen-minute readings using appropriate spreads.

As you gain in experience you will charge accordingly so your prices may not rise as often as other businesses, but you must self-regulate.

Over the months, as your confidence and reputation grow, you will need to think about how you will set about reading in a more private space. I always have a private consultation room in my home that does not interfere with others of the household.

This is not always possible for many reasons. Why?

- Your family may disapprove of what you are doing.
- You do not have the luxury of affording the private space.
- You worry about having strangers come to your home.

To overcome any of the above you could do one of the following:

- Find an alternative lifestyle shop and hire one of their rooms, but be aware that many of these businesses may attempt to have you tone down what you tell their customers. It is most important that you do not jeopardize the quality of your readings in this manner, as Tarot will withdraw its power from you if you do so.
- Continue indefinitely reading from markets or fairs, but get yourself a marquee or tent that affords privacy, as well as a recording device that runs on batteries if electricity is unavailable.
- Let people know that you are willing to travel to their homes. This method is advisable if there is likely to be more than one client at the premises, otherwise the fuel or time could make the venture unworkable and, again, you must price according to your experience.

Prior to acquiring a reputation for accuracy you may encounter discomfort, disbelief—even hostility—from clients, and this is to be taken into account at the onset. You had best develop a thick skin in preparation for the many occurrences where you *will* walk on the edge with your predictions.

It is advisable to have business cards made up with your phone number, e-mail address, and (if appropriate) your website. Many of my clients come from elsewhere in Australia and many come from overseas, so an email address is always handy for them to make long-distance bookings, and many clients will take more than one card so that they can give them to friends or associates.

Advertising can be your own choice, but realize that many people do not want to take the risk of paying money to someone who could turn out to be a charlatan, as does happen, and in many places what you are doing could be classified as illegal.

Under the British Commonwealth law, the Witchcraft Act was repealed in 1951, replaced with the Fraudulent Mediums Act.

Many years ago I lived in the state of Victoria and was subject to a vendetta by a fundamentalist Christian sect that was very influential in the town (at the time). It was a rural area and these people were horrified that I'd arrived and they set about, indirectly (through phone and letter), first threatening the people with whom I and my family were staying, and then, when we moved to our own home, spreading gossip about me and my family.

I had a confrontation with the leader of this group. After going to his home and knocking on the door (he was not at home), I left a message with his wife saying that I wanted to have it out with him, and he could come and visit me on my property if he dared.

He turned up the following day with a Bible and a book of exorcism under his arm, accompanied by another man who said nothing, but whose size and demeanor were intimidating. The first thing the minister said was, "I can't stay long." I invited him to sit outside on my verandah where we talked and debated for the next three hours. He could only see things from his very one-sided theology and I refused to allow him that because, ultimately, I had been initiated into my priesthood before him and could, if playing his game, declare myself senior to him in training.

Ultimately, resolution was futile and at the conclusion of the meeting he informed me that, every Sunday, he and his congregation would "Will me to Jesus or will me dead."

Consequently, when I began working my craft at the local marketplace several weeks later, I was threatened with the cops under the aforementioned act. Nothing eventuated.

Over time, I established myself and was receiving many clients at home. One day a distraught young woman (I'll call her Susie) phoned me, seeking help. She had had a reading from me much earlier. Her husband had been in his early twenties when he had been killed in a motor accident and she was raising their son alone. Her husband's sister was a member of the fundamentalist sect and had loudly proclaimed that Susie was responsible for her late husband's death, declaring that she was in league with the devil because she was interested in all things mystical and had attended meditation classes. The sect, including the infamous minister, had broken into her house while she'd been in town shopping, had ransacked the place, had taken anything they considered suspect, from Linda Goodman's book *Sun Signs* and any other book of its kind, to her Tarot tape (hidden in her underwear drawer), and a pair of Chinese slippers, and had piled them in her backyard and set them on fire.

I suggested she go to the police and have the people concerned charged with breaking and entering and willful destruction of private property, which she did. Nothing could be proven and the charges were eventually dismissed.

Finally the minister was recalled and had to leave the area.

Many years later, after the publication of two books, a well-established clientele, a successful working coven, and workshops on many themes, when I was strongly entrenched in the area, several of us held a Spring Equinox gathering at a friend's very large and well-appointed property that also served as a horse-riding lodge. My friend had cancelled all guests, except for two people, over this particular period and all those attending the ritual gathered with young, potted trees to plant in a grove. It was beautiful.

The following day my family and the coven all left to go on holiday for several days to a beach up the coast. When we returned it was to headlines in the local newspaper.

Another fundamentalist minister had been incorrectly informed that a group of black-clad devil worshippers had gone into the woods carrying a dead horse's head for their evil rites! I was outraged and demanded equal press, to which the newspapers gladly agreed, and I wrote a two-page article on the rites and sacredness of the witch's wheel of the year. I was contacted by a local FM radio and asked for an interview, which I gave, offering the minister the chance to come forward in open debate. The radio loved it and kept the challenge repeated regularly, but the minister went to ground and nothing more was heard from him.

In many parts of the world there are entire communities of fundamentalist religious zealots who would gladly put you to the stake, or use whatever means are available to them to get rid of you, if you are discovered to be psychic or are practicing any of the occult arts, so please take all these things into consideration. I do not mention them to put you off, but simply to enlighten.

Transference

Do telephone or internet readings work? I don't know. There are many variations of clairvoyance and what works for some does not work for others, and these forms of divination do not work for me. I have been asked on several occasions to do remote interpretations, and in my early days I attempted them, but it was dubious whether there was anything of accuracy and so I have dismissed the idea.

Why?

From my understanding what actually happens when a client comes for a consultation is transference. When they sit across the table our energetic fields intermesh and, while remaining very much myself, I also become them. My feelings in relation to events and people become their feelings, who I love is who they will love and who I loathe they will loathe. I know when a situation is distressing or elating because my own body responds to the emotion of the situation so that when, in a reading, I *seem* to give advice or to admonish, praise, or berate, it is because the clients themselves will do so, probably in such a way as to seem to be talking to themselves.

The actual style of the reading will reflect this. I recall one particular example where throughout the session I was subject to very lengthy silences (very unusual for me). The person later went on an around-Australia trek, driving over vast areas of arid landscape, and she informed me that often for hours, if not days, she and her partner said almost nothing.

Transference is such that you will almost always take the viewpoint of the client, despite the little inner voice that informs you that there are always two sides to any situation.

Confusion can come about when the client's views on life are so utterly alien to that of either you or Tarot that you wade through it like molasses. It can be very difficult not to jump up and down on the table in an attempt to educate them on such concepts as self-esteem, individuality, freedom—and at times like those Tarot *will* and *does* interfere in the reading, specifically at question time when there are often no holds barred.

The Code of Silence and Selective Memory

I have been given many peculiar titles over the years but the significant one, in relation to Tarot, is the Mother Superior of Silence.

You are in the same situation as a doctor, lawyer, or priest insofar as you cannot give anyone else information about another's reading. This confidentiality assures clients an intimacy with you that they know can be relied upon. Even when taking calls I rarely record the individual's last name and many do not give it. This ascertains that, on the rare occasion that someone seeks to go through your diaries, your integrity is unchallenged.

Selective memory can be worked on over the years. What is very handy is seeing and knowing way too many people so that, as a general rule, I do not remember people who might have seen me only six months previously.

Several weeks ago I was standing outside a café in town waiting for my daughter while she and her friend went off shopping. During fifteen minutes at least a dozen people passed me saying, "Hi, Ly!" I smiled and returned each of their greetings, but did not recognize any of them.

When the client has been to you on several occasions you may well remember them and some of their details but this is rare, and you set this up on purpose.

When you're "on" you're "on" and when you're not you are most definitely not. You need this objectivity so that when a client comes for a return visit nothing you have seen before interferes in the current session.

First Do No Harm

We now enter into the touchy area of not how much you say in relation to bad news, but the way you say it.

This will tend to change from person to person, but always tell the truth and in retrospect tact isn't one of my greatest virtues (as you will see in later case histories).

The first thing to set up is a reputation for telling whatever you see. If prospective clients phone you and tell you that they do not want to hear anything bad, you will need to give them the choice to go elsewhere. Realize that Tarot *is* a mystical thing and that you cannot put a desire for payment ahead of ethics (and it will always make certain you have food on the table).

This is where reputation is to your advantage over advertising. First of all, it is a rare thing for prospective clients to ever ask me if I'm any good at what I do because they will have heard from friends, family, or colleagues that I *am* good at what I do. On the odd occasion that I am asked that, because a traveler has been recommended to me by a local person or local business rather than someone close to them, I put the question back to them: "Was I recommended?" When they answer in the affirmative I tell them that I will not honk my own horn and that the choice must be to either trust that recommendation or go elsewhere.

Many people, when they first arrive, will shake visibly. They can sometimes be very afraid, but very determined to seek in this Sacred Well. Ignore their discomfort—this technique has the effect of calming them rather than if you were to take notice and seek to comfort them. The phenomenon will soon settle despite what you have to say. The same applies to tears. Both men and women will often cry for no apparent reason (nothing to do with the quality of the news) and often will attempt to apologize, saying that they didn't know what came over them.

Client Contact and the Consultation

From the moment of first contact you will be aware, on some level, that the reading is going to occur; that you are going to dance between the world of time as we know it and the world beyond that which is known. This has already had an impact on both you and the future client.

If taking bookings by phone, you need only secure the individual's first name as, in many instances, the person concerned may require a sense of anonymity, especially a first-timer. I usually ask the person for a return phone number just in case circumstances arise and I am required to cancel with them. If they do not, or cannot comfortably provide this, then we must respect this as their right to privacy.

You will experience a tension (that never goes away) on the days when you are to do readings. I have never fully understood this, but have become quite used to the sensation, realizing that it must have something to do with the constant intention and readiness for the experience. I can also put it down to picking up on the client because most of them will be both apprehensive and excited well before the designated time.

I am always very aware of the need to put the client at ease from the moment they arrive so I am always very friendly and familiar from the outset. I lead them to my rooms and make certain they are comfortable before asking them for their recording device (most still bring cassette tapes although many are now bringing mini-disc devices of their own), which I test to ascertain that it is working.

I then proceed to open my cards (refer to Unit Nine).

You will then pick up the five packs, in any order, and straighten them up before passing them to the client to shuffle. I usually advise the person of the process I have just completed, informing them that the cards are empty and ready to be filled with their own information.

From this moment on you are to be aware of the significance of each spread. It is the *intention* within you that marks each spread's difference. I inform the client, at each phase of the reading, what the spread represents and what events or situations they imbue into the cards as they shuffle.

I would like to add that this shuffling is more than it appears. In Unit One we discussed at length time and DNA. What you are to understand (and I inform many clients of this whenever they ask how it works) is that they don't so much shuffle the cards as sort them into order in much the same way as a virtuoso pianist plays a concerto or a brilliant typist types a document. If the person was to look at the images and attempt to place them in any seeming order they could not do so in the same way as either the pianist or the typist who, if attempting to look at the keys of their instrument while working, could not perform the task. The DNA of the person shuffling has the memory of everything possible within the tips of their fingers and, therefore, they cannot make a mistake. There is nothing random in this process!

You will inform your client that it is your clear intention to keep all events to within a two-year time frame, but that if far-reaching events are triggered within this time frame they will also show up on the table.

When you lay the cards on the table and the prophecy is dire you will need to take a moment to sense how to go about saying what you do. I tend to be a very animated personality so I make faces, swear, ask them to wait a minute, ask them if they really want to hear what I've got to say. I also use humor in such a way as not to offend and will, on occasion, have a sideways conversation with Tarot in front of the person, discussing my hesitance or dilemma. This gives the client a moment to compose themselves, or say they want to go home. Most people are, however, more resilient than we give them credit for and most will tell me to just say it!

So I do.

My first reading of AIDS stands out in my memory. I'd laid the cards on the table and they fell in such a way as to have all the appearance of a television announcement that, in those days, warned people against the disease. So, after several minutes I took a deep breath and told the client I could see the Grim Reaper bowling alley ad on the TV. There! I'd said it!

Instead of an emotional response he smiled at me with such a beautiful smile and informed me that he had full-blown AIDS and just wanted to know how long he had left.

That reading started a progression of these ill men, until I must have read for thousands of them. After seeing the illness many times I became matter-of-fact in seeking to be very honest and help them to prepare in whatever way I could.

At other times I have had to work very hard not to laugh at the enormity of death and destruction I am seeing. One of those times the client relieved me of my anxiety by informing me that she was a paramedic and drove an ambulance in one of the densest and most dangerous places in Sydney, and another was an undercover cop involved in drugs and vice.

It's all okay. Trust and compassion are your greatest tools here and sometimes you will feel moved to work beyond the Tarot table. I have seen instances of child abuse where the children concerned were in the custody of someone else and I have been able to assist the client to get in touch with the relevant authorities; the same applies in instances of domestic violence; or when a parent's offspring has been introduced to addictive substances.

You cannot always help in this manner and must be careful of what is coined "the messiah complex." You need, also, to know that most of the time when there are difficult situations ahead for the individual simply knowing it in advance is the greatest gift you can give them because (a) they are then more ready to deal with the event when it happens and (b) they also know that this event was destiny, the result of which removes a huge amount of unnecessary emotion at the time of the crisis.

Self-Protection and Psychic Clag

Pace yourself. For the first several years I found I was capable of reading for up to five clients a day, at an hour session each, without any seeming personal harm. But it sneaks up on you and if you are not careful your health and well-being will suffer because you are sharing the energy field of every individual who consults you, and traveling time in a strange way.

Case History

The most profound example of directly associated dysfunction was a reading for a friend of mine, a very well-established and respected psychic who held consultations for up to seven hours a day, seven days a week.

Back in those days we read Tarot for each other. I was very upset when I saw in her cards cancer that appeared to be associated with the breasts. I suggested she give up Tarot because the work was taking a heavy toll on her, but she refused, saying she would take her chances.

It was only a few months later that she found a lump in her breast and was diagnosed with the cancer and booked into the regional hospital where the surgeon was to take off the breast and remove the lymph nodes from beneath her arm. She came to see me for a reading before being admitted and Tarot was adamant that she seek another opinion in the city. She did so and was operated on there, where only a small segment of the breast was removed instead of the entire thing.

She seemed to make a full recovery but I was still worried and over time I begged her to stop the readings. After several more scares she did so, opting to return to university and study psychology. She now works in that capacity and the last I heard, which was over a decade ago, she was still healthy.

I also became ill many years ago, diagnosed with asthma. On average, somewhere between ten and twenty people (clients and others) would come through my house each day, and throughout this time I was also raising my children. What happened was that I would have an attack, but as soon as I removed myself from the people around me and went into a room by myself the attack would pass immediately. I began to suspect that I was becoming physically intolerant of people.

When I decided to move to where I now live, I also vowed to slow down with the readings. Now I rarely see more than two clients on any day, and make certain that I take days off in between to have just for myself, to write or to pursue other activities. This has worked for me and I have not had any signs of the disease for many years.

The problem is psychic clag! This stuff can't be seen but can definitely have an affect, just like humidity, just like dust and dust mites. The feeling of this clag is almost indescribable and is almost like static buildup. You will feel off-centre; stale. You will have difficulty concentrating and may also feel listless or depleted. This has nothing to do with the quality of either the reading or the client and the only remedy is to get wet. A shower will do it (*not* a bath), but a dunk in the ocean is by far the most satisfying. Water will neutralize the effect, along with food, exercise, and time alone for a while.

Keeping your workplace clean is also important because psychic clag is a physical thing and has density. Vacuuming your floors regularly, washing the walls, and cleaning the windows will all ensure that your health is kept at its maximum level.

The "He/She's My Best Friend" Syndrome and Personal Privacy

If you live in a small town this can be difficult, because you are likely to connect with clients on a daily basis simply attending to your shopping.

Due to the very private and confidential nature of Tarot you are likely to end up with half the town's secrets and this ensures that many people will want to approach you and fill you in on updates to their situations—if you are not both careful and tactful. I tell people of my well-trained selective memory to avoid this happening where possible, but ultimately I can only be thankful for the many who have filled me in on the eventualities of the prophesies, otherwise this book would not be happening and there would be no case histories to share with you.

The problems arise when people become desperate and (as has happened to me) climb in through an open window of your house at 3 AM, after a domestic situation, seeking solace. They will phone you at any hour of the day or night and it may become advisable to leave the phone off the hook on a regular basis and rely on your answering machine to vet your response to calls.

If you are reading from home you will require a place where people can wait so that they do not walk into your kitchen and think it is okay to sit down and have a chat with your friends and loved ones, as not everyone is aware that assumptions are Mulengro[1].

What's required from you is that you take the responsibility of *being* professional and have clear boundaries. To do this you'll need to constantly update your motive for doing what you do.

"Shoulds": You Won't See What Is Not Realized

Many people think that Tarot is going to get them out of trouble, and first-time clients will often try to tell you—even on the phone when originally making their booking—why they are coming to see you. You must catch them before they do so and inform them that the less you know, the better the reading will be. Most will shut up, but some will continue, saying they are coming because they need Tarot to tell them what to do. Rather than dissuade them from coming it can be advisable, after telling them that that is not what Tarot does, to suggest they attempt to resolve their dilemma before they get to you; that this will allow a clean canvas on which to write the destiny if nothing is clouding their minds at the time of the consultation.

I ask my clients to not even think when they sit before me; to completely relax and to have no expectations based on what they know of their own lives at the moment.

The "shoulds," however, will be inevitable in one out of three people when it comes to the question part of these readings. This is the time for *you*, the reader, to relax and remain detached because Tarot, as a third present entity, will take centre stage and say whatever it deems appropriate because it is never your job to make their deciions for them.

---

[1] See *Witchcraft Theory and Practice*, Ly de Angeles, Llewellyn USA, 2000.

Safety and Responsibility: Some Dos and Don'ts

The first thing to realize if you choose to take on the mantle of Tarot consultant is that you will initially need to have done hundreds of people who are willing to be read, who are willing to remain in contact, and who are willing to provide feedback.

You can, when you are confidently "in the pocket," advertise for clientele, but I advise against it because word of mouth is your most powerful ally, and if you are competent people will talk about you and recommend others to you—and it works, because in over thirty years, with three radical changes of residence, I retain a steady clientele. People will find you no matter where you go, because this skill is something that will always draw them.

You may, in the first few years, enjoy going to others with just such a reputation, but there will come a time when you will no longer require or even want to look into the pool of the future, preferring to wing it because of what you have learned in the first few units. I truly maintain that this is when life becomes exciting beyond all preconceptions.

You will find that it is virtually impossible to read objectively for close friends and family so I suggest you don't even try. If you must experiment, you will require a will of iron to abstain from guessing, or feeling in any way personally involved. The truth of what you see must remain without value judgments.

Make sure clients book ahead—this both psyches you up and allows them time to change their mind.

I only ask the client's first name to allow them to retain their anonymity if they choose. Ask them for appropriate phone numbers if they are booked a long way ahead in case of unforeseen situations occurring.

The recent exception to this rule was on my last trip to Ireland for the pre-release of *The Quickening—An Urban Legend*, whereby, after doing a reading for a friend who spoke to a friend, I was barraged by a large portion of County Connaught and booked by the organizer of my tour for up to six half-hour readings a day for the first two weeks of my stay.

Doing copious numbers of readings will eventually make you very sick. No matter how well you follow the rules of self-protection, a certain amount of other people's energies will still cling to your own field and the emotion involved can severely tax you, because there is *nothing* normal about reading Tarot. You are literally bending the rules of not only perceived reality, but reality in all its unrecognizable guises.

Except for acquiring their star sign to ascertain the card that will represent them (called "the Significator"), do not allow clients to talk to you while you are reading—it will put your objectivity off and you will be unable to read properly for the remainder of the session. Simply ask them at the outset, as politely as you know how, to shut up until section two where they are asked for their three questions.

Do *not* shuffle the cards yourself as you will place some unknown aspects of your own life within the reading and may not know what is yours and what is theirs.

Keep your current deck away from others' hands and dispose of your old, worn pack in a way appropriate to you (you can throw them in the sea or bury them in the garden—just be a little honorable considering how much energy they have accumulated), because the cards themselves will develop a wisdom of their own over time.

There is much superstition regarding the acquisition of a pack of cards and for me the only way is to purchase them myself—that way there will be no doubt of the impartiality of the action.

After reading for the day it is imperative that you shower, bathe, or immerse yourself in an ocean, river, dam, pool, or pond to fully discharge the static build-up that will occur as a result of the readings, and also to rid yourself of *psychic clag,* which is a residual from the clients' fields. You will know what I mean anyway—for the first few years you will feel exhilarated immediately after the sessions, but this is always followed by an uncomfortable exhaustion and dried-out feeling.

The responsibility of reading Tarot is self-evident. You will ride every possible gamut of human experience from great joy to the depths of despair, from drug or alcohol addiction, insanity, domestic violence, and sexual abuse to great love, brilliant careers, and honest spirituality, world travel, and financial wealth. It is in the dark recesses of personal events that you must take the greatest care. You must tell what you see, but you must learn to do so in a way whereby compassion and straight-shooting are combined.

You have a responsibility for maintaining the privacy of each person who comes your way, and are to keep anything said within the sanctuary of your room utterly confidential. You may have a man for a reading for the first hour and his partner for the next, and even though you may very well see the connection you must work as though there is none.

If you tape your readings (and I tape all mine, as there are usually large amounts of information relative to a two-year time span) you must always advise the client to keep their tape private. If they do not it is their business and their choice but in certain cases, where to take a tape home could place the client in extreme danger, I have held on to it on their behalf and they have made time to come and listen to it when necessary.

If you have *any* misgivings regarding anyone who makes contact for a reading, listen to your gut instinct and do not book them!

There is only one instance in my entire life when I have asked a client to leave. He was a pedophile who gloried in his perversity and wanted to take me into his confidence. You have a right to demand that anyone you don't want to read for leave when you request. Do not place yourself in harm's way, because it can happen.

Wrapping Things Up

As I mentioned in the introduction, this has been the book I thought I never would/could write. Just goes to show how constantly one can fool oneself into perceived limitations.

I ask that, when and if the phenomenon that is Tarot kicks in for you, you take care not to burn out.

Even now, after all these years, I take a deep breath when clients are due and sometimes I catch myself toying with the idea of retiring . . . but I figure it doesn't work that way with Tarot, because the phone keeps ringing and the people keep coming.

There is a lot of stress in the world—likely to heat up in the next few decades—and you have the right to say no, to be sick, tired, over it, frustrated at people's anxiety, demands, neediness; to ask that if they have a cold they not come; to be comfortable with taking the phone off the hook.

The way I have taught this in the book form is also, from my personal perspective, a perceived limitation, even though I realize that there are enormous and copious quantities of notes, lists, and concepts.

It has also been suggested to me that I provide more thorough information on the processes and interpretations of each of the example spreads but that is simply not possible. To do that I would need to read each card individually and that is never Tarot because Tarot is also a book. No single word means anything without context and I have purposely attempted to avoid this limitation with examples *so* that you can say, "How does she see that?"

When you look long enough the illusion of separate cards disappears and the story, added to your experiences at the time, will prevail.

The cards in their groupings are a ritual doorway. Other senses are always at play—clairvoyance (clear and psychic sight), clairaudience (clear and psychic hearing), clairsentience (clear and psychic sensory perception), and always when you look at a spread a multitude of other faculties are at work. The dead will rattle you with their incessant desire to let the client know they are around; the Earth herself will speak her pleasure or her pain; unknown people from the future will tell you their names; unborn children will explain to the grieving woman who recently miscarried why they chose not to go through with it at that time, but to be patient; certain gods will get in on the act and choose to teach; alternate selves of the client will tell them all about themselves and the secrets that only they can know.

I have stared dumbstruck when an unsuspecting, first-time client has said, "So, do you just read Tarot?" Like … it's easy? Like being able to look beyond the world and life of individuals or nations and know what will happen and then *having* it happen is the same as cooking spaghetti?

I honor each and every one of you who *get* it; who pass the plateau; who can heal—often without knowing—a distress and a dilemma that is yet to occur because you saw it coming and the person will know the thing was destiny; who have the courage to take the risk of being foolish or a possible failure because what we do is both an art and a science, and it has been disrespected, feared, even persecuted for millennia.

Tarot is like crop circles—the universe's trick; the unraveling of "What ifs" and "Justs" into a paradox of the unanswerable. Its presence leaves us feeling touched by an awesome divinity.

APPENDIX

Meanings with Other Cards

Fool

- With a Court card or the Hermit—a person who will randomly and inadvertently teach the client something of importance, or trigger something of importance, but when the Fool is also in this position the client does not know the person yet.
- With Hanged Man and Moon—it can represent anything from a diving expedition to a person falling from a cliff.
- With 8 of Pentacles, Knight of Pentacles—a professional comedian.
- With 8 of Pentacles, Ace of Cups—an amateur comedian.
- With Ace of Wands, 8 of Pentacles—a satirist.
- With 8 of Pentacles, Page of Cups—this can represent a cartoonist (usually a satirist).

Magician

- With the Significator or a Court card—a person who is self-focused, independent, and/or has a great deal of personal power, individually and/or professionally, and

means the Court card or the client is self-centered (this is a good thing) and self-motivated.
- With High Priestess card—Occult.
- With Devil card—selfishness.
- With Ace of Swords—a control freak. If it falls next to a person it describes their attitude/energy; they will certainly influence the client (for good or ill).
- With Chariot—a person who has passed final exams and is now accredited in their field.
- With events—absolutely new things.

High Priestess

- With 2 of Cups—very hidden.
- With 2 of Cups and a Court card—a mystic, psychic, or magical person.
- With Emperor—formal training in mystical or magical practices.
- With Page of Pentacles—private study in the above.
- With Hierophant—a public figure in magical or mystical practices.

Environmentally:

- With Sun card, 8 of Wands—can represent lands like Egypt, Morocco, Mesopotamia, indigenous desert regions.
- With Hermit card—older mystical regions or sacred sites, usually Northern Hemispheric.
- With Empress card—same as the above but more equatorial.

Empress

- With Moon and a Court card, or even illness cards—hormonal matters for women.
- With Ace of Wands—pregnancy.
- With Hermit and a Court card—an older woman, matriarch (like a grandmother).
- With High Priestess—it represents a very mature, certain-of-her-sexuality woman.

Environmentally:
- With Hermit, and in relation to place—magnificent high places.
- With 8 of Wands—an environment that is agriculturally rich.
- With Moon—wetlands or lush, damp places.

Emperor

- With Justice card—federal law.
- With 5 of Pentacles—welfare.
- With 8 of Wands—local council.
- With 9 of Swords—treatment in a hospital or other orthodox therapy.
- With Star card/World card—cathedrals, old architecture such as the Louvre in Paris.

Hierophant

- With Devil card—more fundamentalist-type religion, potentially dangerous; a religious institution that Tarot dislikes.
- With Justice card—legal marriage of any kind.
- With High Priestess card it can represent more than one thing, and attending cards (and intuition) will be required here: it can represent Judaism (which is matrilineal), or religions or spiritualities that revere a feminine deity or women-of-the-veil, from Islam to Roman Catholic nuns.
- With Chariot—it very often represents Islam.

Environmentally:
- With Star card—it represents places that are known for their religious architecture: Switzerland, Austria, France, Italy, Czech Republic, Jerusalem.

Lovers

- With 7 of Cups—choices are illusions, there is only one way to proceed.
- With a Court card—a person of the sign of Gemini.
- With Page of Swords—the time of Gemini.
- With 2 of Cups—a choice between two lovers or a *ménage à trois*.

Chariot

- With 10 of Pentacles—caravan, bus, house on wheels, temporary dwelling.
- With Emperor—passing exams.
- With Temperance—passing physical examinations.
- With Devil, and any cards of illness or distress it is the end of the period.

Environmentally:

- With Strength—can indicate places such as the Middle East, Arabia, parts of North Africa.

Strength

- With Emperor (also, but in context)—hospitals or the study of physical things.
- With 9 of Swords—physical illness.
- With 10 of Swords—physical pain.
- With 10 of Wands—literally, a heavy load.
- With 8 of Pentacles—body work.
- With 2 of Pentacles—can be a weight-loss program.
- With 5 of Wands—martial arts.
- With 4 of Wands—performance such as dance.
- Falling in the sphere of Netzach on the Tree of Life it can represent sculpture or other very tactile art.
- With Ace of Pentacles—rock solid or non-specific matter.
- With Ace of Wands—I have seen it represent "new matter" for a client who was in the last stages of terminal cancer and wanted to know, from a reading, what would happen after death.
- With Devil card—wild animals, large animal(s), dangerous animals, tainted ground.
- With 10 of Pentacles it can represent a gymnasium or other fitness studio.
- With Moon card and the Page of Cups this card has represented sea creatures such as whales.
- With the Tower it can be either earthquake or blasting as with mining.

Environmentally:

- With Empress card—the equatorial belt.
- With Chariot card—the Middle East.
- Emperor card—England.
- With Sun card—desert land.
- With Star card—America.
- With Sun and Moon cards—oasis-type environments: desert regions with waterways or desert regions around the Mediterranean, such as Morocco.
- With 8 of Wands—a dry, arid region.

Hermit

- With any of the Pages, a wise child or an older child when relevant to several children in a family.
- With Star card and World card—a long way overseas/international.
- With 7 of Pentacles—archaeology, history, or similar.
- With 8 of Pentacles it can be any form of work dealing with that which is old or antique.

Environmentally:

- With 8 of Wands—inland terrain that gets very cold in winter.
- With 6 of Swords—in the case of Australia: somewhere prone to cold like Tasmania or New Zealand (a place surrounded by water but not far off the mainland) whereas in Europe it can be anywhere from Ireland to the Isle of Skye; in the United States it could be Manhattan or any other island off the East Coast.
- With 2 of Wands—Melbourne, Adelaide, New York, Chicago, London, Ontario, Moscow, Zurich, Wellington, Tokyo; a major capital city in a place that gets very cold in winter.
- With Star card—alpine places, mountains, stars on snow.

Wheel of Fortune

- With Knight of Wands, Knight of Pentacles, or Knight of Swords—wheels on vehicles.
- With Devil card—addiction to gambling.

- With 5 of Pentacles—caught in a cycle of poverty.
- With Chariot card/Ace of Pentacles—a win at gambling.
- With Empress—a yearly or planting cycle.
- With Moon—a lunar cycle.

Justice

- With Emperor card—federal and local government.
- With 5 of Pentacles—bankruptcy.
- With Devil card—enforced control, illegal graft, corruption.
- With 8 of Swords—imprisonment or entrapment.
- With 10 of Pentacles—the contract relating to a rented or leased dwelling.
- With 10 of Cups—the contract or deed of ownership on the sale or buying of a home.

Hanged Man

- If Death is present in a spread it can be martyrdom/assassination.
- With 3 of Swords—separation: no point fighting; rejection or dismissal of any kind.
- With Moon card—diving or fishing.
- With Death card/10 of Swords—can represent the victim of a murder or a suicide by hanging or strangulation, or being pushed off a high place.
- With Fool card and the 4 of Wands—can represent extreme sports such as bungee-jumping or abseiling.
- Similarly, with the Star card and any pleasure cards—parachuting, hang-gliding, any aerial sport or high circus activity.

Death

- Star/Tower/Death—represented the destruction and resulting deaths of September 11, 2001.
- Devil/Tower/Death—appeared just prior to the London bombing in 2005.
- 5 of Swords/Tower/Death—preceded the war between Israel and Hezbollah/Hamas 2006.

- With Chariot card—passing tests or exams.
- With 5 of Swords, Ace of Swords—war.
- With Moon card—failure.
- With 8 of Swords—a stalemate.
- With Ace of Swords—a natural physical death.
- With 10 of Swords—violent death. Can indicate self-inflicted by self-injection and overdose as in the case of addiction; messier types of death, violent accident. Don't be fooled . . . I have had the same with the 8 of Pentacles (the woman was an ambulance driver in inner-city Sydney).
- Ace of Swords, 9 of Swords, Death card—the contemplation of death/suicide.
- With the 5 of Cups—mourning.

Temperance

- With Magician card—can represent a person involved in alchemy, or alchemy itself.
- With Emperor card—it can represent medication or medicine.
- With Emperor card and the 10 of Pentacles—a medical practice (physical or psychological), a pharmacy or drugstore.
- With a King or Queen—can represent a doctor, pharmacist, chemist, someone involved in medical research.
- With Devil card and a Court card—can represent a recovering addict or alcoholic.
- Also with the Devil card, where there is no indication of a person, or addictive situation, and often with the 9 of Swords—a sick person on some form of traditional medication.
- With Ace of Wands—verbal exchanges; the dialogue process.

Environmentally:

- With 8 of Wands—plains or large tracts of farmland.

Devil

- With 6 of Pentacles—corruption/bribery.
- With Knight of Pentacles—problems with car or finances.

- With 7 of Pentacles it can represent either a marijuana crop or a form of physical cancer.
- With 4 of Pentacles a thing is stuck, not moving.
- With Knight of Wands it is dysfunctional communication or major travel delays.
- With Ace of Swords—fear of violence or the ability to commit violence.
- With 8 of Wands—the person will need to be careful in relation to property or property dealings; it can also represent poisoned land through chemical use or otherwise.
- With Queen or King of Pentacles—often a Capricorn woman or man.
- With Strength—if shown in an environmental sense it can represent caves or dangerous, deep places; it can also represent dangerous animals, usually large (with the Moon card it can represent such things as sharks). If shown in a health spread it can represent deep infection or chronic diseases of the bone or joints.
- With Strength and Emperor—dictatorships.
- With Strength, Tower—mining explosions; strip-mining; can also represent nuclear meltdown.
- With Moon card—clinical insanity.
- With Moon card and the 8 of Wands it can be someone who works with the psychologically disturbed.
- With Moon card and the Emperor this card can represent asylums or psychological institutions.
- With 7 of Cups—delusional behavior.
- With 10 of Swords—deep pain, extreme violence or violation.
- With 5 of Swords—domestic violence, a dirty fight, terrorism.
- With 2 of Cups—sexual abuse, fear around sex, sexually transmitted disease.
- With 9 of Swords—insomnia, long-term illness.
- With 6 of Cups—heavy drug use.
- With Hierophant—extremist religious ideology or deeply dysfunctional marriage.

Tower

- With Ace of Wands—literally: a fire.
- With Star card—satellite or plane crashes to earth; can be missiles in a war scenario.

- With Strength card—rock explosion as in open-cut mining; a bomb.
- With 5 of Swords—individually: huge argument; large scale: violent street protest; military clashes.
- With Moon card—meltdown, inner explosion; can be a person or a nuclear reactor; can be violent storms.
- Tower/Moon/Star—severe weather patterns.
- In Chokmah in a Tree of Life layout—electricity danger of some kind.
- With Page of Wands and Tower (anecdotally)—I recall watching Australian Idol in 2005 and one episode showed the contestants having their Tarot read. I watched as the central theme for one of the contestants was laid out with these two cards crossing each other, and I knew immediately that her voice was going to "go." Three weeks later she was struck with an acute virus affecting her throat but she still sang. The judges applauded her knowing how ill she had been all week. She went on to win the competition.

Environmentally:

- Empress/Strength/Tower—New Zealand or places of high cragged mountains usually volcanic or on fault lines.

Star

- With Pentacles—technology or technological projects; also scientific.
- With 7 of Swords—a commitment of over seventeen years.
- With 10 of Swords—broken glass.
- With World/Star—long-distance flights.
- 8 of Pentacles—can represent an astrologer.
- With Sun—can represent astrology itself.
- With Strength—can represent gemstones.
- With Ace of Pentacles—long-term investment; can also represent scientific knowledge or breakthroughs, especially if attended by the Emperor.

Environmentally:

- With 3 of Wands—a coastal place, usually in a clear, warm area.
- With 2 of Wands it can represent any West Coast city.
- With 10 of Pentacles, Emperor—an airport.

Moon

- With Empress—women's bodies.
- With Page of Cups—creatures of the sea (not mammals).
- With 4 of Wands—Full-Moon parties.
- With 9 of Swords—worry or depression; insomnia or other sleep-related dysfunctions.
- With 8 of Pentacles—can represent night-shift work.
- With 4 of Swords—boredom; the frustration of waiting.
- With Ace of Wands—communication difficulties or misunderstandings, or, conversely, deep levels of communication. The difference will depend on surrounding cards.
- With 2 of Cups—sexual disappointments or naivety.
- With 6 of Swords—a boat, surfboard, or other water-craft.

Environmentally:

- With 10 of Pentacles it can represent a sauna or an indoor swimming pool or plumbing.
- With 2 of Swords—ocean frontage.
- With 8 of Wands—lakes or large inland bodies of water.
- With Devil, 2 of Swords—dangerous waters or dangerous, unseen things below the surface.

Sun

- With Star card—astrology.
- With Ace of Wands—a biological birth.
- With Ace of Pentacles—wealth.
- With activities cards this always represents successful outcomes.

Environmentally:

- With Strength card—hot, dry, stony places.
- With Empress card—hot, moist places.

Judgement

- Obscurely, with the Page of Wands—dental work.
- With Empress card—can represent the seasons of a year.
- With any activities cards (such as the Wheel of Fortune)—expect changes, delays or re-directions.
- With Death—the changes are complete (for now).
- With Moon—changes of mood; changes of mind.

World

- With 6 of Swords—long overseas journey.
- With Star card—the internet, information technology, international flight.
- With Emperor—international affairs and organizations like the UN.
- With Ace of Pentacles, Emperor—large financial institutions such as the IMF.
- With 5 of Swords and/or the Strength card it can represent a world war.

Environmentally:

- With 10 of Pentacles—can represent any kind of community centre.
- With 10 of Pentacles, Emperor—the dwelling-places of government or organizational bodies.
- Can literally be: the World.

Ace of Wands

- With Star card—internet; media.
- With 10 of Wands—written research or compilation.
- With Empress card—pregnancy.
- With Sun card—birth.
- With Tower card—fire or explosion.
- With 5 of Wands—a musical band or a dance troupe.
- With Page of Wands—a letter or any mailed document.

Environmentally:

- With Ace of Wands, 10 of Pentacles—can represent a publishing house, or a library.

2 of Wands

- With 10 of Cups—the/a person's home is, or will be, in a city.
- With Court cards—a person who is at the top of their field.

Environmentally:

- With 8 of Wands—inland cities.
- With World card and other significant place cards—major capital cities somewhere else in the world (a travel card—like the Knight of Wands: light-hearted travel, or the Knight of Pentacles: travel for practical or business purposes—would most likely fall close by, often with the Star card indicating flight).
- With Strength—London, Glasgow, or Edinborough.
- With Strength, High Priestess—Jerusalem or other major Middle Eastern or North African cities.
- With Ace of Pentacles, Star, High Priestess—Kuwait or Dubai.
- With Ace of Pentacles, Star—any extremely prosperous capital city.
- With Star, Hermit—cities such as New York, Zurich, all major cities in Alpine countries.

3 of Wands

Environmentally:

- With 2 of Wands and the Hermit card—a city that is cold in winter.
- With 8 of Wands and the Hermit card—an inland city that is cold in winter in the same country as the client.
- With 6 of Swords and the Hermit—an island off the mainland of the country of the client—never very far, also that gets cold in winter, somewhere like Tasmania off Australia, New Zealand, Victoria Island off Canada, Long Island off New York, USA, the Isle of Skye off Scotland.
- With 2 of Wands and the Empress card—a more-or-less tropical city in the same country as the client.
- With 8 of Wands and the Star card—the West Coast of the country of the client.

4 of Wands

- With 2 of Swords—a surprise party.
- With 10 of Pentacles—opening a shop, restaurant, gallery.
- With Ace of Wands and the 8 of Wands—an outdoor party.
- With 5 of Wands—bands, music, live performance.
- With Moon card—modeling for the fashion or image industry, television.
- With 8 of Pentacles—a person who works in the hospitality industry.

5 of Wands

- With Emperor card—red tape, bureaucracy.
- With 5 of Swords—industrial disputes, strikes, protesting.
- With Queen, King, or Page of Swords it can indicate a Gemini.
- With 9 or 10 of Wands—mess to be picked up.
- With Strength card—physical discipline like martial arts.
- With 10 of Pentacles—building materials for an unfinished house or house being renovated.
- With 7 of Cups—false communication, Mulengro.
- With 8 of Wands—multiple occupancy or community/company title land.

6 of Wands

- With Emperor card—always school teacher.
- With Star card and the 5 of Wands—internet chat, email or communication.
- With Knight of Wands and the 7 of Wands—a person speaking many languages.
- With Ace of Wands—a public speaker or public speech.
- With place cards—where a phone call is to or from.
- With 10 of Cups and cards indicating the buying or selling of real estate—an auction.

7 of Wands

- There are no consistent correlations.

8 of Wands

- With 5 of Wands—multiple occupancy, community or company titled property.
- With Ace of Swords—subdivisions, boundaries, or fences in relation to rural land.
- With 5 of Swords and the Ace of Swords—struggle over borders or boundaries (can be local or international, as this sequence has shown up in relation to the dispute over territory between Palestine and Israel).
- With 8 of Swords there will be difficulty with access (road or driveway).
- With Emperor—local councils or government lands departments.

Environmentally:

- With 2 of Wands—a small coastal town.
- With Empress—rural but tropical environments.
- With Strength—arid landscapes.
- With Hermit—cold, dry climates.
- With Empress, Strength—desert land, but lush like Kakadu National Park in Australia.

9 of Wands

- With Ace of Wands, 8 of Pentacles—can represent a writer of some description who either has writer's block, or is having their words censored in some way.
- With any relationship cards there is communication imbalance.
- With Justice card and any other cards representing legal situations—the person to whom the pattern refers is not speaking, or refusing to speak.
- With illness cards (such as the 9 or 10 of Swords)—can represent laryngitis, tonsillitis, or some very uncomfortable throat disease.

10 of Wands

- With the Emperor card—any form of research.
- With the 10 of Pentacles—can represent a house being built of wood or moving to a new rented or leased dwelling.

- With the Empress card—can represent anything from the responsibilities of motherhood to being a busy chef.
- With the Strength card and a Court card—literally represents a physically strong person.

Knight of Wands

- With 7 of Wands—a letter, phone call, public speaking.
- With Star card—airmail/e-mail.
- With Ace of Wands—language.
- With Emperor—learning a language or the study of literature or like subjects.
- With Page of Wands (not a child)—communication, a small to medium-sized package or a letter on the way.
- With a Page (a child in this instance)—a child who is talkative and able to communicate easily.
- With Moon card it is internal dialogue, psychic or intuitive communication.
- With 10 of Wands and the World card—backpacking.
- With 10 of Swords—can represent a car accident where damage is incurred.
- With the 9 of Wands—can represent writer's block or an inability or lack of desire to communicate.

Page of Wands

- With Strength—time or sign of Leo.
- With Sun—time or sign of Aries.
- With Temperance—time or sign of Sagittarius.
- With Ace of Wands—books or publications.
- With 8 of Pentacles—working with words.
- With 4 of Wands—a production has begun; a creative venture has begun.
- With Moon—descriptive art of any kind.
- With Tower—sudden, acute illness affecting the throat.
- With Knight of Wands or Knight of Pentacles—a communication device such as phone or letter (not internet or e-mail—that would require Star somewhere close by).

Queen of Wands

- With Temperance—quite likely to be a Sagittarian.
- With Strength—quite likely to be a Leo.
- With Emperor (or, without any logical reason, Chariot or Magician)—quite likely to be an Aries.

King of Wands

- Same meanings as the Queen of Wands, above.

Ace of Cups

- With 8 of Pentacles—for the love of work; work that one loves or amateur work (vocation).
- With Page of Cups and Hierophant—can mean Roman Catholic religion: a brief description of a past event similar to this was seeing 8 of Pentacles, Ace of Cups, and Hierophant. I was at a momentary loss and I mumbled aloud "This doesn't make sense unless you're a priest!" The man answered that he was a Roman Catholic priest who also had an interest in all things mystical, even Tarot, and was involved, unbeknownst to his peers, in a magical order.
- In all other instances it defines love.

2 of Cups

- With the 8 of Pentacles—can represent the sex industry: the first time I ever realized this was when the 8 of Pentacles fell in the sphere of Netzach on the Tree of Life. The client was a madam who ran two brothels in Melbourne! The person concerned could as easily sell luxurious, sexy underwear.
- I have had this card with the Emperor and Ace of Wands for an academic who writes books about sex and sexuality.
- With Devil card—can represent devious sexual behavior.
- With Devil and the 9 of Swords—can represent sexually transmitted disease.
- With Judgement and any of the Pages—can represent the transformation into puberty.

3 of Cups

- With Empress and 4 of Wands—a women's festival or party.
- With 8 of Pentacles—can represent friends or family in business together.
- With 10 of Pentacles—can represent people sharing a rented house or apartment.
- With Knight of Wands and distance cards—represents either people traveling together or people meeting up at a designated destination.

4 of Cups

- With 3 of Cups—reunion, but with unforeseen and additional events involved.
- With 3 of Pentacles—an interview that will result in perks not initially seen. Same applies with 8 of Pentacles.
- When in conjunction with 10 of Cups or Pentacles and Justice—indicates offers relative to contractual arrangements and alternative opportunities.

5 of Cups

- With Moon, 4 of Wands, or 5 of Wands—can represent The Blues (as a form of musical expression).
- With Death—traditional mourning.
- With Hierophant or 2 of Cups—indicates past failed relationships or repeat letdowns in a single relationship.
- With Moon, 9 of Swords—depression or remorse.
- With Justice—can indicate the loss of a prolonged legal case (the 3 cups mean that there would have been more than one instance of appearance, appeal or application).

6 of Cups

- With 3 of Cups—a reunion.
- With Moon—things of the past can have a psychological effect on the person or can be the cause of disillusionment.
- With Emperor—can represent archives or old-fashioned people.
- With 8 of Pentacles—indicates work within an arcane field such as history, archaeology, genealogy.

- With 8 of Cups, Wheel of Fortune—a return to past work.
- With Hierophant—a past marriage.
- With 2 of Cups—a past relationship.
- With 4 of Wands—a reunion or reunion party.
- With Ace of Wands, Page of Wands, or Knight of Wands—information or documentation pertaining to the past; historical books.

7 of Cups

- With Devil—addiction.
- With Moon—mental illness.
- With Moon and 8 of Pentacles—a person who works with the people diagnosed with mental illness.
- With Moon and Emperor—the institution or places of learning associated with mental illness.
- With Ace of Wands or Page of Wands—an imaginative process (or the idea) such as writing a fictional book or story.
- With Ace of Wands and Page of Cups—an impressionist work of art or a work of art not based on traditional portrait or landscape.
- With Ace of Wands, Strength card—the idea for any form of 3D art such as sculpture or decoration.

8 of Cups

- There are no consistent correlations with the 8 of Cups—you will determine the circumstances by whatever it falls with.

9 of Cups

- If falling with a Court card—the person concerned can be either a very happy person, a buffoon, or a pompous person.
- With 10 of Swords, Devil—a situation where cruelty gives pleasure.
- With Devil, 2 of Cups—a situation where deviant sexual extremes give pleasure.
- With Devil, 4 of Wands—can represent gluttony or "a part-drug event."
- With Devil, Strength—obesity due to gluttony.
- With Devil and many other cards—a range of self-serving self-indulgences.

10 of Cups

- With Justice—can be contracts of sale.
- With Justice, 8 of Swords—delays or constraints concerning contractual property deals.
- With 10 of Pentacles, Death (or the 9 of Cups)—the completion of construction of a house.
- With 3 of Cups—a family reunion.
- With Moon, 9 of Swords—there are likely to be plumbing or water problems,
- With Emperor and Tower—disaster will occur that involves insurance of home and contents issues.
- With 7 of Swords and either Moon or 2 of Swords—there are thieves in the area of the person's home.
- With 8 of Swords and any inauspicious cards—the person concerned is likely (for whatever reasons) to be house-bound.

Knight of Cups

- It is of detriment when it shows up with Moon and 7 of Cups—opiate-based drug abuse.
- With 4 of Wands—an invitation.
- With 7 of Cups—the offer is untrustworthy or comes to nothing.
- With Hanged Man and 9 of Swords—can be a person who gives too much and is easily hurt.

Page of Cups

- With Death card—time or sign of Scorpio.
- With Moon card—time or sign of Pisces.
- With Chariot card—time or sign of Cancer.
- Also with Moon—can represent visual arts.
- With Moon, Emperor—it can represent the study of art but with 7 of Wands it is still study (or teaching) but not necessarily through a traditional institution.
- With Hierophant, Sun—Roman Catholicism (see Ace of Cups).

Queen of Cups

- With Moon—quite likely to be a woman of the sign of Pisces.
- With Chariot—quite likely to be a woman of the sign of Cancer.
- With Death—quite likely to be a woman of the sign of Scorpio.

(The above will depend very much on other attending cards).

- With 6 of Swords, 10 of Pentacles—can be a woman of the sea: a yachtswoman or a woman who lives on a boat.
- With 6 of Swords and 4 of Wands—a surfer or someone who gains pleasure from the water.
- With 8 of Pentacles and Ace of Cups—can be anything from a swimmer to a swimming coach to a plumber, but a professional.
- With 8 of Pentacles, Empress—can be a midwife.
- Can sometimes represent a medical doctor if around the Temperance card or the Emperor card.

King of Cups

- All of the meanings given under Queen of Cups, above, can also represent this card.

Ace of Pentacles

- With Ace of Wands and an accompanying Knight—new matter.
- With Strength—rock solid, solid rock, stone, foundations (as in a building).
- With Sun—material wealth.
- With Justice—money gained through legal means (the sale of property, for example).
- With Emperor—can represent a government grant or a scholarship.

2 of Pentacles

- With Ace of Pentacles—a large sum of money (in the client's considered opinion), or settlement, divided between two or more parties.
- With 10 of Pentacles—shared accommodation.

- With 10 of Pentacles and Moon—sharing shop fronts or displays.
- With 8 of Pentacles—part-time or casual work; can be unstable employment or financial situation: things can go either way.
- With 2 of Cups—friends or lovers who share financial things in common.
- With Moon, 7 of Cups—can represent bipolar dysfunction.

3 of Pentacles

- With 8 of Pentacles—a job interview.
- With Emperor and Temperance—can represent a medical consultation.
- With home or dwelling cards such as 10 of Pentacles or Cups, accompanied by cards such as 10 of Wands, Moon, 5 of Wands—can represent either the building of a place or work/renovations being carried out on a place. The 3 of Pentacles, in this instance, is the client discussing the plans with the trades people.
- With Justice—discussions of a legal nature.

4 of Pentacles

- With Ace of Pentacles—a deposit or part thereof.
- With Strength—body fat or obesity.
- With Moon—fluid retention.
- With a Court card—a miser or someone holding on very tightly to what they have.
- With High Priestess—hidden money or possessions; same with 2 of Swords.

5 of Pentacles

- With Strength—can represent such dysfunctions as anorexia or bulimia.
- With 7 of Swords and Moon—a theft.
- With 8 of Swords—indebtedness that one cannot escape, or a heavy fine.
- With Devil—poverty or financial loss due to obsessive or unwise spending.
- With Moon—poverty of mind; poverty of emotion; entrenched poverty.
- With Emperor and Ace of Swords—can represent departmental or governmental cuts to funding of any kind.

- With Tower and 10 of Pentacles—can represent crashes on a stock exchange (large or small).
- With Justice—extreme court or legal costs.
- With Temperance, Emperor—it can represent the state of having no health insurance due to lack of money.

6 of Pentacles

- With 8 of Pentacles—can represent either the wages paid or a person who pays wages.
- With Magician and a Court card—can represent a person who patronizes or belittles others.
- With 5 of Pentacles and a Court card—can represent a person who values themselves badly or feels/is impoverished by others.

7 of Pentacles

- With Devil and 4 of words—a controlled or dormant cancer.
- With Devil and other relevant cards—any plant crop considered illegal: anything from marijuana (which is commonly seen) to opium poppy and coca.
- With 3 of Swords and Devil—the removal of a possibly dangerous or carcinogenic growth (mole or tumor) but can as easily be warts. Cards surrounding it will imply the severity of the condition.
- With Devil and Empress—rampant growth such as occurs in tropical locations; or unwanted growth such as happens with an unwanted pregnancy, mould, fungal infections; infestations of any kind.
- With 8 of Pentacles—work in a growth industry.
- With Pages as children—growth spurts or a rapidly growing child.
- With Strength—a person may put on large amounts of weight.
- With Wheel of Fortune—annual or seasonal growth.
- With World—can indicate population growth.

8 of Pentacles

- There are no necessary correlations—it simply means work, and its interpretation will depend on the circumstances.

9 of Pentacles

- With 8 of Pentacles, Ace of Swords—an editor of some kind.
- With 10 of Cups or 10 of Pentacles—a dwelling that is small but Zen.
- With a Court card—a person of refinement who has nothing to prove.
- With Ace of Wands (and perhaps Page of Wands)—a publication with no extraneous or unnecessary embellishment to make it appealing.
- With the Ace of Wands, also—clear, concise communication.
- With the Ace of Wands this can apply to any form of art or business.
- With Star—advertising (sometimes) that does not insult the public.
- With any of the Knights—quality transportation or a journey that is short but satisfying.

10 of Pentacles

- Can be a house of knowledge if attended by Emperor or cards of study and learning.
- With High Priestess—a place of the study of the occult.
- With Temperance—indicates a place where the healing arts are studied.
- With Page of Cups and Temperance—it can indicate a place where visual arts are studied.
- It is not the 10 of Cups, but can become so—an incomplete dwelling.
- With Emperor—houses where money moves: banks, credit companies; also government departments and such places as schools or hospital buildings.
- With Knight of Pentacles—caravan, bus, mobile home.
- With 5 of Wands and 10 of Wands—a dwelling being built.
- With 2 of Pentacles—a shared rental/house; a shared business.
- With Strength—building societies, gymnasiums or other sporting establishments.
- With Strength, Temperance—places where physical disciplines or therapies of an alternative nature are conducted.

- With Strength, Emperor—military buildings.
- With Justice—a courtroom; the signing of leases or property contracts.
- With Page of Cups—Blue Chips; sure things on the stock market.
- With 6 of Swords—houseboat, yacht, launch, or ship.

Knight of Pentacles

- With 10 of Wands—carrying heavy loads.
- With 2 of Pentacles—part-time financial venture.
- As a form of transportation it is a larger vehicle such as a 4-wheel drive, a bus, or a train.
- With 8 of Pentacles—the process of one's work or someone who works with money or within a financial institution.
- With Justice—the paperwork.
- With Ace of Wands (sometimes Knight of Wands or Page of Wands)—a large parcel or package.

Page of Pentacles

- With Empress card—the time or sign of Taurus (not Hierophant).
- With Devil card—the time or sign of Capricorn.
- With Hermit card—the time or sign of Virgo.
- With Knight of Wands and the Wheel of Fortune—craft or food markets; fairs.
- With Strength—a big kid or an adult behaving like a big kid.

Queen of Pentacles

- With Empress—quite likely a woman of the sign of Taurus (not Hierophant).
- With Devil—quite likely a woman of the sign of Capricorn.
- With Hermit—quite likely a woman of the sign of Virgo.
- With Strength—a very physically fit woman.
- With Ace of Pentacles—a wealthy woman . . . please bear in mind that the term wealth is sometimes conceptual rather than literal, it will always be determined by the client's concept of wealth.

- With 5 of Pentacles, 9 of Swords (or 10 of Swords if severe)—a person with a physical disability such as arthritis or osteoporosis.
- With 7 of Pentacles—a gardener or woman who likes to garden.
- With 8 of Pentacles and 10 of Cups/Pentacles, a woman in real-estate or a woman who works from home.

King of Pentacles

- All of the Queen of Pentacles meanings also apply to the King.
- With Strength though, sometimes in difference to a woman—a very big guy: strong rather than obese, although if either the Devil card or the 5 of Pentacles falls with it, that could change the pattern of physicality (same for the Queen).

Ace of Swords

- With 7 of Swords—bound to a commitment and can't get out of it.
- With 8 of Wands—boundaries around land or property.
- With 8 of Wands and Lovers—subdivision of property.
- It can literally represent a sword as it occurs within traditional martial arts.
- With Emperor, 5 of Swords—it can represent a soldier, his or her training, his or her weapons or war itself.
- With a Court card the person depicted is quite likely to be an authority but that would depend on the cards around it because, add a 10 of Swords to this and we have either back pain or cruelty.
- With 8 of Pentacles the situation changes again. An example would be King of Swords, Ace of Swords, 10 of Swords, 8 of Pentacles, Temperance—this man is in the business of healing utilizing, such skills as acupuncture, osteopathy, or chiropractics, for example.
- With Death—death.

2 of Swords

- With Star and any slight medical or health issues—can indicate eyesight problems or things to do with limited vision.
- With Moon—it can represent living by, or being near, the ocean or a large body of water.

- However, with Moon, 7 of Swords—looks to me like a thief is sneaking around by night!
- With 10 of Cups or 10 of Pentacles—a dwelling out of sight to the general public.
- With High Priestess—no matter what else is around it, this is a "double-up," indicating strong psychic situations or people.

3 of Swords

- With Tower or other cards of ill-health—heart attack or related illness.
- With Tower, 10 of Pentacles—the demolition of a building.
- With cards indicating surgery (major or minor)—the 3 of Swords is the process of whatever is removed from the body.
- With Hierophant—marital separation.
- With 2 of Cups—separation between lovers.
- With Empress, 9 of Cups—a baby born.

4 of Swords

- This represents waiting and stillness. There are no multiple correlations necessary here.

5 of Swords

- With 5 of Wands/Emperor—industrial dispute or strike.
- With Devil—drunken, or drug-related violence; domestic violence.
- With Tower, Death, or any of the Dark-Night-of-the-Soul cards—violence, war, and/or battle, from local to international.
- With Ace of Wands, 3 of Cups—debating or debating societies.

6 of Swords

- With Court cards—surfers, divers, or people who fish (with the Hanged Man).
- With Knights of Wands or Pentacles—boats, boat travel, or medium-to-large watercraft of any kind.
- With Knight of Swords—fast-moving things on or in the water.

- With Moon and 8 of Pentacles—a professional fisher.
- When Death is assured—it is not going to happen for a long time.
- With World—long international journeys.
- With 10 of Pentacles—houseboat, a water vessel on which one can reside.

7 of Swords

- With Moon—someone spreading rumors.
- With 5 of Pentacles—loss through theft.
- With Emperor card—can indicate anything from a governmental body planning in secret to graft or corruption.
- With Devil and 9 of Swords—can indicate a virus or bacteria (can't be seen) that will make someone ill.
- With 8 of Pentacles—either a person who is a snitch in a work situation, a lazy person (Devil card) at work who is avoiding their job through subterfuge, a person who is working on the sly, or a person working a black-market job.

With Court cards the variation is enormous:

- Court card, Justice—undercover police or agency of some description.
- Court card, Justice—the opposite applies: a criminal avoiding justice.
- Court card, Emperor—a spy or intelligence agent.

8 of Swords

- With Justice—can indicate anything from a legally-binding contract, to imprisonment, to losing a driving license for some illegal reason.
- With 8 of Wands—stuck somewhere without transport.
- With Star—a commitment lasting for upwards of seventeen years (like parenthood); delays or cancellations around airports; computer or network failure.
- With Moon, 9 of Swords—sleeplessness or insomnia (chronic).

9 of Swords

- With Emperor, Temperance—the health industry.
- With 8 of Pentacles—night shift.

- With 8 of Pentacles, Temperance, or Emperor—a nurse.
- With the Moon card—insomnia, bad dreams or nightmares.
- With 5 of Wands, Page of Cups, Moon—singing the blues.
- With Ace of Wands (and other Wands and/or Knight of Pentacles)—working on a speech.
- With Court cards it is either of detriment or advantage, depending on the nature of the person. Some people work things out by so-called worrying at them.
- With Strength, 10 of Swords—physical pain.
- With Death, 5 of Cups—bereavement.
- With 7 of Cups—worry over what will not even eventuate.

10 of Swords

- With 8 of Pentacles/Ace of Swords—a person working in any field such as: tattooing, piercing, acupuncture, chiropractics.
- With Star—stabbing pain in the eyes (vision); injury from broken glass.
- With Judgement, Page of Pentacles—toothache.
- With 3 of Swords—heart attack; radical severance.
- With Death—violent death.
- With Death, Hanged Man—violent, extreme suicide such as would be for suicide bombers.
- With 5 of Swords—war-inflicted (of whatever kind) injury/pain.
- With Emperor, Devil—torture.
- With a Court card, Devil—either a person being violently abused … or the abuser (torturer).

Knight of Swords

- With 10 of Pentacles—a mobile phone.
- Can represent a vehicle with two wheels—bicycle or motor bike.
- With a Court card—either an aggressive, quick tempered, and/or impatient person or a person who moves swiftly in whatever circumstance shows itself.
- With Star—quick or short flights.
- With Knight of Wands or Chariot—fast cars.

- With Strength and any Page—fast horse or horses; race horses.
- With Magician—brisk, no-nonsense people.
- With Devil—amphetamine-type drugs or cocaine.
- Also, with Devil and financial gains (Ace of Pentacles, 7 of Pentacles) or losses (5 of Pentacles) this card relates to horse-racing as a gambling addiction.
- With 7 of Swords, Justice—lost driver's license because of speeding.
- With many of the Wands—fast words, short stories, articles, people with quick tongues—often thoughtless.
- With a Page (a child, in this instance)—hyperactive or one unable to do things at a steady pace.
- With Justice card and other auspicious cards—a quick resolution to a court case.

Page of Swords

- With Queen of Swords—a young woman, usually fair skinned and/or blonde.
- With Lovers—the time or sign of Gemini.
- With Star—the time or sign of Aquarius; ideas, the thinking process.
- With Ace of Swords—also ideas.
- With Justice—the time or sign of Libra.
- With Strength—an animal; pale animal.
- With the Ace of Wands—inspiration, thoughts.
- With Knight of Pentacles—intellectual pursuits.

Queen of Swords

- With Justice—quite likely to be a Libran.
- With Star—quite likely to be an Aquarius.
- With Lovers—quite likely to be a Gemini.

King of Swords

- See Queen of Swords.

Annotated Bibliography

Badcock, C. *Evolution and Individual Behavior: An Introduction to Human Sociobiology.* Oxford, Blackwell, 1991.
> This text looks at human behavior beyond androcentric blinkers, causing the reader to consider our own species in relativity to all others.

Campbell, J. *The Masks of God—Occidental Mythology.* Penguin Books, USA, 1964.
> Beginning his exploration of myth and religion with "The Age of the Goddess," Campbell leads us from Mesopotamia and "The Serpent Bride" to Minoan Crete, and the beginnings of the rise of patriarchy in the Age of Heroes; from the Levant to Europe, from Persia to Hellenism; the Roman period including the Celtic provinces through to the rise of Islam to a resurgent Europe and the concretization of Christianity in the modern psyche.

Campbell, J. *The Masks of God—Primitive Mythology.* Viking Penguin Inc., 1959.
> Campbell explores the role of mask, image, and imagination, the origins of humanity's concepts of "supernormal" and the contemporary relationship to superstition and the sacred through the Ages of Man, culminating in "The Function of Myth on the human psyche."

Chown, M. *The Universe Next Door*. Headline Book Publishing, UK, 2001.

>Chown raises questions such as "can time run backwards?" and he delves into the weird and wonderful, challenging theories of science. This work is called "cutting edge." The Foreword "The Making of Tomorrow's Science" sets the stage for part 1 "The Nature of Reality," which discusses time (what it is and is not); whether a time machine is possible; the existence of alternate realities and many worlds and what constitutes alien life.

Deutsch, D. *The Fabric of Reality*. Allen Lane, Penguin Press, 1997.

>The author's view on quantum theory is based on his idea about parallel universes. Some people will love it, others won't.

Eisler, R. *The Chalice and the Blade*. HarperCollins, USA, 1987.

>This book discusses the effects of what Eisler calls a "dominator culture" on current humanity. The author, with degrees in sociology and law, gives a feminist approach to history and social behavior. Her work has inspired the Center for Partnership Studies, USA http://www.partnershipway.org.

Gibran, Kahlil. *The Prophet*. Alfred A Knopf, Inc., 1923 (136th printing, 2001).

>This is a series of spiritual discourses on almost every subject from love and children to pain and death, that has inspired me for decades

Gleick, J. *Chaos: Making a New Science*. Heinemann Publishing, USA, 1988.

>Ever heard the term "Butterfly Effect?" As this book says in the prologue: "Believers in chaos … feel that they are turning back a trend in science toward reductionism, the analysis of systems in terms of their constituent parts: quarks, chromosomes, or neurons. They believe that they are looking for the whole."

Hawking, S. *A Brief History of Time*. Bantam Books, UK, 1988.

>This bestseller provides theories and possible explanations to such big questions as "wWhere did we come from?" and "why is the universe the way it is?"

Huntington, S. P. *The Clash of Civilizations and the Remaking of World Order*. Simon & Schuster, USA, 1996.

>This book theorizes that an age of ideology has ended; that the primary axis of conflict in the future will be along cultural and religious lines.

Margulis, L and D. Sagan. *Mystery Dance: On the Evolution of Human Sexuality*. Summit Books, NY, 1991.

>"The cooperative hunting groups that began with Homo erectus—our most recent evolutionary predecessor—ushered in relatively high levels of sperm com-

petition." This book takes a look at why we, as a species, behave as we do and create sexual paradigms consistent with many other species.

Quinn, D. *Beyond Civilization*. Three Rivers Press, USA, 2000.

Daniel Quinn was first known through print with his enlightening novel "Ishmael." *Beyond Civilization* suggests a future tribalism—the result of our currently unsustainable cultural model.

Reanney, D. *Music of the Mind*. Hill of Content, Australia, 1994.

Can we *literally* be on different wavelengths when unable to understand each other? Posing many questions regarding life and death, and what else both could be, Dr. Reanney mixes poetry, philosophy, and narrative together with solid scientific theory; one of my favorite thinkers.

Reanney, D. *The Death of Forever—A New Future for Human Consciousness*. Longman Cheshire, Australia, 1991.

"Easily recognizable images based on familiar things have given way to abstract theorems which tell of particles moving backwards in time, of a universe structured in eleven dimensions, and so on. During this process, the status of common sense has been inverted: no longer our guide in the search for truth, it has become our adversary." Initially this book comes across as exactly the opposite of the title … and it took me three attempts to get into it. By the third chapter I was hooked and have since re-read it several times. Dr. Reanney speaks *with* his readers.

Robertson, J. M. *The Nag Hammadi Library*. Harper, USA, 1988.

These texts, discovered in Upper Egypt in 1945, are a selection of Gnostic works dated from the first century CE. Their very existence challenges mainstream religious ideology and concepts of creationism.

Saul, J. R. *On Equilibrium*. Penguin Books, 2001.

Saul identifies six qualities that give humans the ability to act responsibly: common sense, ethics, imagination, intuition, memory, and reason. Saul suggests that people have the ability to shape events rather than be shaped by them.

Silva, F. *Secrets in the Fields*. Hampton Roads Publishing Company, USA, 2002.

Explores the mystery of crop circles.

Thomas, D. *The Poems of Dylan Thomas*. New Directions Publishing Corp., USA, 1952.

Recommended Reading and Internet References

De Angeles, L. *Witchcraft: Theory and Practice*, Llewellyn Worldwide, USA, 2000.

Fortune, D. *Mystical Qabalah*, Samuel Weiser, USA, 1984.

Hand Clow, B. *Chiron*, 2nd Ed, Llewellyn's Modern Astrology Library, Llewellyn Worldwide, USA, 1999.

Perera, S. B. *Descent to the Goddess; A Way of Initiation for Women*, Inner City Books, Toronto, Canada, 1981.

Regardie, I. *A Garden of Pomegranates*, Llewellyn Publications, USA, 1970.

Regardie, I. *The Tree of Life*, Samuel Weiser Inc., USA, 1972.

Bernard Casimir—http://www.celtic-casimir.aunz.com/home.html.

Ly de Angeles—http://www.lydeangeles.com.

Internet Encyclopedia of Philosophy—http://www.iep.utm.edu/t/time.htm.